"Anyone who has experienced family trauma and struggles with reconciling such relationships with the life they know they deserve will benefit greatly from reading this book. Harris's frank and gracious approach is grounded in an inspiring personal journey that reflects the power and freedom—and challenges—that come when we finally decide to tell the truth."

—**Nicola A. Menzie,** Founding Editor, *Faithfully Magazine*

"Every once in a while, a book comes along that reveals things you didn't even know were hidden. With the skill of a surgeon, Harris extracts brokenness and brings hope. When it comes to family heartache, the typical response is to ignore or excuse, but this book invites us to another option . . . to get free. A must-read for anyone serious about moving from pain to possibility."

—**Gari Meacham,** President and CEO, The Vine Uganda, and author of *Spirit Hunger, Watershed Moments, Truly Fed*, and *Be Free*

"Like a loving friend, Harris opens readers' eyes to ideas about family and loyalty that offer life-changing insights for Christians who have experienced family trauma. Through her approachable and vulnerable style, she validates those who have struggled with caring for themselves amid family turmoil and clarifies how the Word of God helps us understand family and forgiveness. Harris presents a clear image of God and family that is a liberating must-read."

—**Stacie Craft DeFreitas,** PhD, LSSP, clinical psychologist and author of *African American Psychology: A Positive Psychology Perspective*

"Courageously transparent and daringly vulnerable, Dr. Harris shares her personal experiences with family trauma and her journey toward liberation. The biblical truths she expounds uplift and encourage those of us from broken families that wholeness is indeed possible."

—**Reverend Dr. Jonathan Chism,** author of *30 Day Journey with Martin Luther King Jr.*

"It is evident from the very first word, first sentence, and first page that Dr. Sistah Felicia Harris's book *First in the Family* is a one-of-kind remedy for the wounded and broken-hearted seeking relief from God for wounds untold. She bears her soul as she revisits the past to impart wisdom and hope into the present and future of the reader. Each page drips with authenticity and vulnerability, which is an essential sacrifice for those of us who follow Christ. Dr. Harris provides us with a road map to peace and joy that we are all seeking in one way or another. I pray that God will use this book to speak to his children to let them know that the shackles that bind them to generational curses can and will be broken! After reading this book, they will have the confidence and strength to walk boldly into the promises of God!!"

—**Dr. Tina M. Harris,** Professor and Endowed Chair of Race, Media, & Cultural Literacy; Affiliate, The African and African American Studies Program, Louisiana State University, Manship School of Mass Communication

FIRST
IN
THE
FAMILY

FIRST IN THE FAMILY

Biblical Truths for Cycle Breakers

FELICIA HARRIS

LEAFWOOD
P U B L I S H E R S

an imprint of Abilene Christian University Press

FIRST IN THE FAMILY

Biblical Truths for Cycle Breakers

LEAFWOOD
P U B L I S H E R S
an imprint of Abilene Christian University Press

Copyright © 2021 by Felicia Harris

ISBN 978-1-68426-361-5

Printed in the United States of America

Cataloging-in-Publication Data is on file at the Library of Congress, Washington, DC.

Cover design by ThinkPen Design | Interior text design by Strong Design, Sandy Armstrong

Leafwood Publishers is an imprint of Abilene Christian University Press
ACU Box 29138
Abilene, Texas 79699

1-877-816-4455
www.leafwoodpublishers.com

21 22 23 24 25 26 27 / 7 6 5 4 3 2 1

CONTENTS

1   NOT ALONE 11

2   FIRST IN THE FAMILY 23

3   DADDY ISSUES 45

4   WITHOUT HONOR 69

5   MY GOD WILL RESCUE 91

6   FALLING OUT 115

7   BEAUTIFUL FUTURES 139

Afterword   OVERCOMERS 165

Acknowledgments 173

*I dedicate this book to my mama
and my son—and the countless people
doing the difficult work to pursue
beautiful futures and create abundant
lives in a fallen world.*

NOT ALONE

> *Blessed be the God and Father of our Lord Jesus Christ,*
> *the Father of mercies and the God of all comfort. He*
> *comforts us in all our affliction, so that we may be*
> *able to comfort those who are in any kind of affliction,*
> *through the comfort we ourselves receive from God. For*
> *just as the sufferings of Christ overflow to us, so also*
> *through Christ our comfort overflows.*
>
> **2 Corinthians 1:3–5**

I'm not supposed to be writing this.

Chances are, you feel as if you are not supposed to be reading this, even though your heart leapt at the idea of pursuing hope and healing for family bondage or brokenness that you have been praying about for years. I know that the mere thought of someone seeing this book in your hands, and what it suggests, may be nerve-racking for you. However, I promise not to take it personally if you choose to hide this book as you read it, because I may or may not be hiding as I write it.

I'm well aware (as I'm certain that you are, too) of the pressure our culture places on us to have happy, healthy, and whole families.

Families that function without trauma, darkness, suffering, or loss.

Families that have a mother, and a father, and 2.5 children born exactly 18 months apart.

Families that eat around the breakfast table and pile onto the couch on Friday evenings for movie nights.

Families that read the Bible together, pray together, and have Sunday dinners after church.

But chances are, this ideal family is not your family. And by now, as you have probably guessed, it is not mine either.

Instead, my family was torn apart at the seams when my father committed a heinous act under the guise of darkness and the influence of alcohol in the room of one of my older siblings, while another sibling watched him tiptoe back and forth from the shadows of the hallway and through the bedroom door of a child.

My mother's world was rocked upside down when she had to grapple with the reality of this type of evil and betrayal in her marriage, and, though she hated the idea, divorce was the answer. Although my parents did a brief stint in therapy, the pain and anger were too raw and overwhelming to endure. My father was out of our lives, and suddenly, my mother was a single parent of four children and an ex-military wife trying to make ends meet.

My mother worked endless hours at countless jobs while my siblings and I stayed home alone, learning how to fend for ourselves while adjusting to our new family dynamic. At the same time, my older siblings found themselves in new roles of responsibility, looking after each other and the house in the aftermath of the shock and brokenness caused by a sexual assault, while we all tried to "make do" with the circumstances and pick up the pieces of our lives. But those broken pieces continued to shatter even more, and in the decades that have passed, my family has endured homelessness, poverty, drug and alcohol addiction, imprisonment, physical violence, and more.

Does any of this sound familiar? The unspeakable happens—infidelity, divorce, rape, death, murder, abandonment, job loss—and instead of confronting family trauma head on, the decision is made to simply search for the silver lining, grin and bear, and wait for the suffering to subside. Then, in what feels like the blink of an eye, years have passed, and instead of subsiding, the suffering seems to have spread to every area of your life.

An all-too-common yet ineffective strategy, "making do" in the wake of this kind of trauma, and the suffering and darkness it creates within our families, is a dangerous coping mechanism that offers our enemy a foothold, allowing him to blaze a trail of bondage and brokenness that can impact generations. But it does not have to be this way. This raises the question: Why is it that we are willing to boldly confess to so many areas of sin and spiritual warfare in our personal lives, but when it comes to our families, we are more prone to suffer in isolation, silence, and shame?

I believe it is because so much of our family story is tied up in tangled bows with other people whom we love more than anything in the world, and we want to avoid things getting messy. It may be one thing to confess our own sins and deal with the consequences of our individual mess, but when that mess is connected to a parent, a sibling, or a relative, things get a bit more complicated. And intimidating. As a result, the interconnected nature of family that was designed to wrap us in love and support can instead leave us feeling bound and stuck.

This is why family trauma and the resulting brokenness and bondage are both pervasive and infectious.

As a child, it was hard for me to understand the brokenness from which my mother was operating, doing her best to make ends meet and push our family forward from one day to the next. It felt as if the sins of my father and our trauma were a secret that was everywhere and yet nowhere to be found. We pushed it down because we did not know that we had the power to drive it out. But the fateful reality is that this sort of trauma does not simply disappear, and it does not stay put.

Without carving an intentional pathway to freedom, the brokenness and betrayal we experience within our families become open doors for our enemy to wreak havoc on every family member, from parents to toddlers. I was only two years old the night my father tiptoed into the bedroom door of my older sibling, but his drunken moment impacted me all the same.

What happened that night set off a chain of events that resulted in years plagued by loneliness, anger, rejection, isolation, and fear for every member of my family. And while I wish I could say that that chapter has closed and all brokenness has been mended, unfortunately, that is not the case. But—and this is the good news in the midst of what may feel like a tragic story—I found a hope in Christ that conquers trauma and reminds me of the overwhelming love and abundant life he prepared for me well in advance of placing me in the graces of my family of origin.

> For we are his workmanship, created in Christ Jesus for good works, which God prepared ahead of time for us to do. (Eph. 2:10)

Now, I am no family guru, but I am a woman who has made it a part of my personal ministry and mission to dispel the lies we believe about family. That's because I see how much bondage and complacency come along with our sense of duty and the pain we experience in trying to protect the secrets and the status of the ones we love. My hope compels me to share this good news and my testimony with you: God can mend broken hearts and redeem broken legacies—that is, if we are willing to surrender our plans and desires for our families to him.

When I began to seek God and his Word for answers to the difficult questions that I had about moving forward in the face of all that my family has endured, I begin to experience peace and clarity for the first time in my life. I learned that I was not alone. In fact, I learned that not only was God with me, he was for me and intimately interested in every detail of my life, including the ones that I falsely believed I could not share with anyone else. Once I finally surrendered my family's story to God, everything changed.

And now I am writing to encourage you that your story does not have to end the same way it began, either. The gospel of Christ and the promises and truths shared in Scripture offer guidance for understanding how to navigate the complex relationships within our families of origin. You may be surprised to discover that Scripture often deviates from the picture of family perfection that our culture relies on to convince us that nothing stands above the name of family.

That picture of perfection that we've been told to look up to is a narrative that fails to confront the reality that our families are made of imperfect people. And placing our hope in imperfect people will never compare to placing our hope in Christ—and Christ alone. Unlike people, he never fails. This is the reason we pray in the name of Jesus and not in the name of family.

Make no mistake—the story I am telling is not an assault on the institution of family. It is impossible to deny the role that healthy, happy, and whole families serve in the development of healthy, happy, and whole people. And those people are blessed beyond measure. But for once, this story is not about those people or those families.

This story is for people who struggle to find the blessings in their families of origin. This story is an invitation to people who need hope and healing for the brokenness that may have occurred at the hands of the people who the world told them were supposed to love and protect them at all costs, but instead they did not. I am telling this story so that people who come from unhealthy, unhappy, and broken families do not have to go on to live unhealthy, unhappy, and broken lives.

I am telling this story because some families are messy. And some families do harm. Don't believe me? Just open your Bible.

Cain murdered Abel.

Joseph's brothers threw him into a pit and left him to die.

Sarah abused Hagar, who was the mother of her husband's son.

Jacob tricked his father so that he could steal his brother's birthright—and his mom helped him pull it off!

David was initially overlooked by his father and brothers and then left in a field to tend sheep. Years later, David's son, Amnon, fell in love with and raped his sister, Tamar, only to be murdered by his brother, Absalom. That's a story of abandonment, rejection, incest, rape, murder, and estrangement—all in one family alone.

And those stories are just off the top of my head! As destructive as these tales may sound, every single person mentioned here still served a purpose in God's plan.

So, no, I am not writing an assault on the institution of family, but I am writing to offer hope and a defense against the lies that Satan whispers about our duty, our worth, and our futures when we find ourselves confronted by the reality of a family of origin with imperfect people. Because these stories are much more common than we have been led to believe, and they can be found almost anywhere you look.

For years, I have heard these stories while standing at the altar and praying alongside members of my church. Person after person staying behind for prayer after service on Sundays, standing in front of me with the weight of their brokenness on their shoulders, weeping and asking for God to intervene in their family's circumstances.

In my role as a college professor, I have heard these stories from first-generation students who encounter battles with their families when it comes time to carve out a plan for their lives. The pressure to perform and make everyone proud pushes up against the hope and passion they possess for their own lives. I have watched students struggling to drudge through the fallout of making a decision to preserve their future at the expense of the approval and support of someone they love dearly. Here, the weight of responsibility and legacy and duty and honor joins with the fear of failure and rejection and regret.

We hear the embarrassing family arguments of our neighbors. We see the toll that family blowups take on the lives of our friends. We see the consequences of family conflicts all around us. And we cannot deny that oftentimes, family drama—and trauma—wreak havoc on our lives.

This family stuff is complicated.

Still, when you are in one of these stories, it is not unusual to feel that your suffering is hiding right in plain sight. Somehow, along the way, our culture has offered us mixed signals: when it comes to our families, it is our duty to make peace with the worst, but we should idolize the best. A confusing message indeed.

The good news is that in the midst of what feels like absolute chaos, God still hears you—and he sees you, too.

This is the promise made clear in Hagar's story when, after being forced to bear a son by Abraham and endure abuse from Sarah, she finds herself alone in the wilderness, not once but twice: once when her circumstances were so unbearable that she tried to run away, and a second time after Abraham and Sarah bore a son of their own and forced her and her son to leave. During both of these family crises, the angel of the Lord appeared to comfort Hagar. When she tried to run away, the angel told her that God had heard her misery. When she was forced to leave, the angel told her not to fear. In the midst of this brokenness, Hagar gave God the name El Roi, declaring that she had seen the one who had seen her (Gen. 16–21).

The story of Abraham, Sarah, and Hagar is a dysfunctional family tale if we have ever heard one, but it is one that gives us reason to hope. Not only was God able to fulfill his plan for Abraham and Sarah's lives in spite of their doubting and conspiring; he did so while acknowledging the pain that their disbelief had caused Hagar, all while orchestrating and fulfilling a plan for her life, too.

That's the thing about God: nothing, and I mean absolutely nothing, gets wasted.

This is a promise for those of us reeling from broken and imperfect families yet desiring to grow in purpose and live in freedom. God shares our desires. He says in his Word that he desires for us to live abundantly; this means he calls us to live a life free from fear, guilt, shame, condemnation, confusion, and any of the sin that entangles us and prevents us from running the race that he set forth for us (Heb. 12:1).

But make no mistake, dear reader. Satan does not want you to read this book for the same reason that he did not want me to write it. Accepting the falsehoods of rejection, loneliness, and trauma that entered your life—oftentimes by no fault of your own—is the perfect web of deceit for the enemy, whose ultimate goal is to distract you from your purpose, if not utterly destroy it.

Our enemy wants you to believe that the divorce, the molestation, the rejection, the addiction, the mental illness, the poverty, the loneliness, and the rest are simply the way it is and the way it will always be. He knows that so many of us will justify our brokenness and betrayal in the name of family.

Oftentimes, there's nothing we would not do for family, even if it means sacrificing ourselves. It is an uncomfortable truth, but the culture-driven mindset of "family first" has been successful in keeping so many bound in circumstances that chip away at their hope and dim their light. Even believers find themselves caught up in this web. God's will is for us to live free, yet our enemy plots to use our love and desire for ideal families to oppress us. Thank God the enemy has been defeated, and you and I can move forward in victory and freedom from the evils that seek to destroy us and our families.

Now, I have to be honest with you. This will not be easy. The stories shared within these pages are as hard to read as they were to write. But I am confident that there is power in knowing that the body of Christ suffers together. And, dear reader, we cannot cease suffering until we are equipped to confront the lies and schemes of Satan with life-altering truths and God-breathed promises found in his Word.

God understands that families can be devastatingly dysfunctional. Yet, for every devastation, God offers unwavering love and the promise of hope for a future. When we allow the guilt and shame of not having an ideal family to render us powerless and longing for what could have been or what *should* have been, we end up plastering a smile on our silent suffering and become vulnerable to the traps and pitfalls of a cultural obsession that is not biblically accurate.

In the pages ahead, we will uncover what God reveals about the nature of family in his Word and place it head to head with today's culture-driven pressures on family life.

God desires for you and me to live an abundant life that he prepared for us long before we were born into our families, and every moment we buy into the lies of our enemy regarding our family circumstances is robbing us of the peace that God so freely gives.

So, although I am not supposed to be, here I am, quite possibly hiding while writing to you. If I am being honest, I am trembling, just as the apostle Paul describes when he originally approached the church at Corinth (1 Cor. 2:3). But I know this is a good tremble—one filled with hope that this book will be a declaration of God's wisdom, healing, and supernatural, restorative power, so that your faith may not rest in my insight or the telling of my story, but on God's power at work within these pages.

You are my brother and my sister and my mother. And, even if you are hiding as you read, I hope you find comfort in knowing that God sees you exactly where you are, and he has ordained our meeting here in these pages. You are not alone. I know that his Spirit is among us, and beyond that, I am grateful for his promise that where his Spirit is there is freedom.

FIRST IN THE FAMILY

> *Then I heard the voice of the Lord asking:*
> *Who will I send? Who will go for us?*
> *I said: Here I am. Send me.*
> Isaiah 6:8

Not too long ago, I learned that I am what people in therapy circles refer to as a "cycle breaker." This type of person is someone who works to end an unhealthy pattern, or cycle, in their family, such as abuse, addiction, or poverty. The reason there's a term for this type of person among therapists is because there is often an incredible fallout when you decide to be the first person in the family to take the path toward freedom and healing, as opposed to placing your family first and ahead of your individual mental, emotional, and spiritual needs. We'll address the issue of fallout later. For now, I want to explain a bit more about what it means to be a cycle breaker and how this decision impacts our relationships with our family members and our lives.

A cycle breaker is a person who would confront an abuser, regardless of their standing in the family. They refuse to continue mismanaging finances in order to keep up appearances for others. They openly protect their children from the toxic parenting traditions of grandparents and aunts and uncles. They consistently, and unapologetically, refuse to perpetuate harmful behaviors, patterns, and attitudes, even when it means confronting the people in their lives they love the most. This can be awfully difficult, and many cycle breakers find themselves in need of mental, emotional, and spiritual support. Thus, the person who is likely to end up sitting on the therapy couch, balling their eyes out while clenching a tear-stained tissue, is the person who values healing the most, but not necessarily the person in the family who needs the most healing.

I know I just told you in the previous chapter that you are not alone, but I want to affirm you, just as any therapist treating a cycle breaker would: this *feels* incredibly lonely. When you make a decision to question or disrupt things that have always been, it rarely goes over well. Thankfully, my earlier truth still stands: even when you feel lonely, remember that you are not alone, and trust that the experiences and emotions you endure as a cycle breaker are shared with believers in similar circumstances every day.

For example, many women experience overwhelming feelings of angst and loneliness when they become new mothers. The best practices around parenting seem to be evolving every year, and each new generation of mothers is met with conflicting knowledge and tips from both the medical community and the community of mothers who support them in their transition to motherhood. As a result, new moms are forced to decide if they are going to trust the science, trust their loved ones, figure it out on their own, or come up with some other option that is a combination of all three choices. Honestly, it's all very nerve-racking, no matter how prepared you think you are.

I'll never forget the disagreement I had with my son's grandmother over a persistent face rash that looked concerning. He couldn't have been more than a few weeks old, and I was in the state of frantic helicopter parenting that required every decision to be informed by the medical community found on Google. One day, she asked me what I was going to do about the rash, and I told her that I had scheduled a doctor's appointment. She scoffed and told me that I simply needed to place my son's wet diaper on his face. This was an old home remedy that she and the aunties swore by, but it sounded completely ridiculous to me. When she expressed her displeasure at my unwillingness to try it her way, I doubled down on my decision, noting that while I was grateful for the wisdom and assistance she was offering, I preferred to wait on the medical advice of my son's doctor. At the appointment, the doctor confirmed that the wet diaper method was an old wives' remedy but noted that a dab of hydrocortisone would be just fine. So, that's what we did.

This disagreement was a notable one because it was the first time that I stood up to my son's grandmother and challenged her parenting advice. It was also the first time that I had the courage to do what I felt was best for me and my son, without looking for the approval of others. Initially, I was beating myself up for challenging an elder, and I worried about how it would impact our future interactions. However, once I saw how quickly and efficiently the dab of hydrocortisone worked, I gained confidence in my ability to trust my judgment and do things differently when it came to what I knew was best for my son.

Although this was not a significant fallout by any means, many can relate to a memorable moment when you decided to go against the grain, no matter how uncomfortable it was, and do things differently for the first time. It can be frightening and lonely, and the anxiety is only exacerbated by the fear that you might be offending someone you love. However, something on the inside of you compels you to create your own path. While this path may not be comfortable, it is the path that God has called you to embrace. This is the recurring dilemma of a cycle breaker.

Discernment Made Me Do It

What I did not know at the time of my son's alarming facial rash was that the gnawing sense of confidence encouraging me to dare to do things differently—even with very little reason to trust my own judgment in a completely new arena of my life— was called *discernment*. Discernment is a spiritual gift that guides our assessment of information and other phenomena that influence our lives, whether it be advice from the elders or biblical statements made from a pulpit. It's the feeling that settles down in the pit of our stomach and says, "Something about this isn't exactly right or true; perhaps you should not trust this completely," or "There is a different way to go about this—a better way that will resonate more with you specifically."

Discernment compels us to make decisions according to God's will for our lives, free from the influence of external factors that govern much of the world's decision-making, such as public opinion, culture, media, false prophets, or—you guessed it—family. Although it can be easy to confuse discernment with the popular notion of intuition, it's important to note that spiritual discernment is much more than magically knowing what to do. It is a process of spirit-led judgment that leads us to know what is right:

> Do not be conformed to this age, but be transformed by the renewing of your mind, so that you may discern what is the good, pleasing, and perfect will of God. (Rom. 12:2)

Discernment is a key tool in the arsenal of any believer, but an especially potent one for cycle breakers. When we feel the strong pull to break away from the harmful routines, behaviors, and attitudes that are embraced by those around us, this is often a sign that we are being called by God into something more: something good and acceptable and perfect. Now, I'm not talking about simple decisions like choosing not to treat a face rash with a wet diaper. I'm talking about the pull to do the even bigger and scarier things with consequences that are even more intimidating than a rift with a grandparent (although that can be quite intimidating).

I'm talking about being the first in your family to move away and attend college or pursue your dream job. The first to choose to cut off all communication with a toxic relative. The first to abandon holiday traditions to create new ones that are healthy and affirming. The first to question if your family is enabling someone's addiction out loud. The first to leave your family's historical church to try a nondenominational place of worship, complete with smoke machines and weird concert-style lights during the announcements. The first to establish healthy boundaries around your time, money, energy, or input.

The pull to make these bold decisions might start as a tiny inkling in the back of your mind, but over time, it grows stronger and stronger until you can't deny that this is your discernment and not a fleeting thought. I've felt that pull ahead of every decision that made me "first" in my life, and even when a decision was a difficult one to make, the results have always been something that surpassed my wildest dreams and deepened my faith in God's ability to make a way for me, even when everything around me was encouraging me to shrink back into a world of complacency and comfort.

Just like going out on a limb for a crazy dream, honoring our discernment is a personal decision that can be difficult to explain or justify to others. We simply know that we are being compelled to do things differently. As I have grown in my relationship with God over the years, I've learned how to trust my discernment more and to step out in faith toward where God is leading me, even when I know there might be backlash for my personal decisions. Throughout this process (and on those therapy couches), I have learned that oftentimes the backlash we experience from loved ones is a reflection of unresolved hurt in their own lives—and not our own wrongdoing.

You have probably heard the saying "Hurt people hurt people." Well, family, I have to break it to you just as my life experiences broke it to me: our loved ones are not exempt from that truth just because we love them dearly. Unfortunately, it is likely that when you make a decision to break an unhealthy cycle, you will be made to feel that prioritizing what's best for you is selfish, inconsiderate, and cruel. In turn, after your initial attempt to step out and become the first person in your family to carve his or her own path, it can be easy to second guess if the dream or pathway you are pursuing is worth the potential backlash. If this is where you are, I hope you find comfort in knowing that you are exactly where you are supposed to be. How do I know? The backlash is your evidence.

Remember that enemy who wants to destroy your purpose and rob you of the calling God has for you? Convincing you to second guess your discernment is one of the tools in *his* arsenal. Sadly, Satan will use anything and anyone to lure you into a state of complacency that doesn't get in the way of his plans for your life (because, just as with God, our enemy has a plan for us too). Oftentimes, he uses the lure of comfort, hallmarked by the allure of total peace and harmony with those who are important to us, to accomplish his goal of distraction or deferment. And he does this because he knows you'll never get to the promise God has on the other side if you don't embrace discomfort and trust your discernment.

On the Other Side of Family

Even if things get ugly—and there is a chance that they will—honoring the dreams and discernment we receive from God places us in a position to fulfill his will for our lives. And because God works in miraculous ways that our brains cannot possibly conceive, his will coming to fruition in our lives can also be an influencing factor that impacts the very people who shunned us for choosing to do things differently. I cannot think of a better example of this principle at work than in the lives of Joseph and his eleven brothers, who threw him into a pit, then sold him into slavery, and left him for what they presumed would be an untimely death. Care to join me for story time?

After detailing a long history of tragic sibling rivalries marked by murder (Cain and Abel), abandonment (Isaac and Ishmael), and manipulation (Jacob and Esau), the book of Genesis saves the ultimate family showdown for its final chapters, chronicling the story of Joseph in Genesis 37–50. Joseph, who received blatant preferential treatment as the favorite of Jacob's twelve sons, was a dreamer. Alas, Joseph did not simply dream and keep his interpretations to himself; he boasted to his brothers about the dreams God gave him, which caused tension among them.

Upon realizing that Joseph's dreams implied that he would one day reign over them and they would bow down to him, his brothers devised a plan to kill him while out grazing their father's flocks. Their jealousy was to the point that they hated Joseph because of his dreams (and his boasting, I'm sure). In fact, when they saw him approaching them in the distance, the Bible says they mockingly exclaimed, "Oh, look, here comes that dream expert!" (Gen. 37:19). Their plot to kill Joseph was a direct attempt to stop his God-given dreams from being fulfilled. However, after some internal debate, the group decided that maybe shedding blood was a bit too extreme. Instead, they settled on throwing him into an empty pit while they discussed the situation further over dinner. Serendipitously, a caravan appeared on the horizon, and the decision was made to sell him into slavery instead. After all, they agreed, he *was* their own flesh and blood.

As ridiculous as the plot of this story reads, the sad truth is that many can relate to Joseph's abandonment all too well. In our enthusiasm, or maybe our ignorance, we boast about the plans and pathways God has revealed to us for our lives, and instead of being met with encouragement and love, we are met with envy and malice. To make matters worse, our experiences can be exacerbated when we dare to rejoice in the midst of a situation that is already warped by dysfunction.

I am almost certain it did not help Joseph's case that his father, Jacob, had so openly favored him in front of his brothers, gifting him with items such as an elaborate robe and creating an environment where Joseph's brothers most likely felt like they needed to do something dramatic for a chance to earn their father's attention and approval. It wasn't just Joseph's arrogance and dreaming that inspired his brothers to plot against him; it was the entire dysfunctional family dynamic. Joseph's brothers were already dealing with their unresolved hurt. His bragging about his noble future was just the cherry on top.

After being sold into slavery by his brothers, Joseph's story gets worse before it gets better—and then it gets worse again. Upon arriving as a captive to Egypt, he prospers as a slave for Potiphar, one of Pharaoh's highest-ranking officials. That is, until Potiphar's wife attempts to seduce him and he denies her advances. In turn, she accuses him of rape, and he is thrown into prison. There, Joseph finds favor again, yet waits in captivity for years before he is called to assist Pharaoh with the interpretation of a dream. Yep, the same gift that caused him grief among his brothers is the gift that grants him favor and results in his ability to advance into a position of great service and value to Pharaoh.

It's in this position that Joseph is able to impact the lives of not only the entire nation of Egypt, but his brothers and father as well. When a famine takes hold of the land, Joseph's guilt-ridden brothers appear in Egypt, seeking provision. In spite of his earlier betrayal, a clearly conflicted Joseph is not only able to provide food for his family; he is also able to move his father and brothers, and all of their belongings, from the barren land of Canaan to the *best* part of the land in Egypt (Gen. 47:11–12). After Jacob dies, Joseph's brothers fear that he might finally pay them back for abandoning him into slavery. However, Joseph reminds them that, though they meant to harm him, "God intended it for good to accomplish what is now being done, the saving of many lives" (Gen. 50:20 NIV).

Oftentimes, we hear Joseph's story taught as a lesson on dreaming, or jealousy, or favor, or provision in the midst of abandonment. However, what sticks out to me the most is the vastness of God's purpose for what would happen on the other side of Joseph's tumultuous conflict with his family. Every single aspect of this family's dysfunction, from Jacob's pref- erential treatment of Joseph, stirring up jealousy among his children, to the last-minute decision made by Joseph's broth- ers to merely sell him into slavery instead of murdering him, was used to fulfill God's will—his good and acceptable and perfect plan that spared the lives of countless Egyptians and Joseph's entire family, preserving what would later become the tribes of Israel. The story of Joseph gives me hope because it offers three truths to remember when conflicts with my loved ones grow turbulent and I'm faced with feelings of rejection, betrayal, or isolation.

You don't have to be perfect to be "first." In spite of some of the accusations you might receive from others that choosing to do things differently means "you think you're better than everyone else," Joseph's story reveals that you don't have to be perfect or better than anyone to become a crucial component in God's master plan. You simply have to be willing to be used by God to fulfill the plan that he has for your life. The notes in my study Bible refer to Joseph as a brat who felt like he was entitled to the preferential treatment he received from his father. But even Joseph's own arrogance did not discount that the vision he received from God in his dreams was accurate.

As Joseph continued to trust God on his rollercoaster of highs and lows, we see the nature of his character progress into a humble servant eager to be used in whatever capacity needed, whether as a slave or a prisoner or a royal official. Every step of the way, we read that the Lord was with him, showing him kindness and granting him favor (Gen. 39:21). By the time Joseph was called upon to interpret Pharaoh's dreams, his prior perspective of his own noble status has been completely transformed, and he humbly acknowledges that it is only by the power of God that he is able to give Pharaoh an answer to the questions about his dreams (Gen. 41:16).

Still, Joseph is no saint. When he is confronted with the arrival of his brothers after years of separation, he struggles to move past their conflict. He doesn't immediately reveal himself to be their brother or absolve them of their sins. Instead, he plays tricks on them, tosses a couple of them into prison, and has them traveling back and forth to Canaan to fulfill trivial requests. This process draws out until finally, in a flurry of emotions, Joseph can no longer keep up the façade and comes clean. In this series of events, Joseph's humanity is on full display. Though it is evident that he loves his brothers and does not wish to repay them with harm, it still takes him a while to arrive at forgiveness. Based on his actions and the revelation that his brothers still questioned his motives up until the final chapter of this story, we can only imagine that even after the family reconciled, the relationships were tense. But that's okay because it reveals another truth about being first.

God's favor is not dependent upon having good relationships with your family. One of my favorite scriptures in the Bible that appeals to my little sliver of pettiness that still needs deliverance states, "If it is possible, as much as depends on you, live peaceably with all men" (Rom. 12:18 NKJV). Granted, verse 17 says not to repay evil for evil, and verse 19 reminds us that vengeance belongs to the Lord. Still, there is something about the apostle Paul using that double-pronged introduction that lets me know that he knew that sometimes it is not possible—and sometimes it has nothing to do with you that it isn't possible—to live at peace with others. Yes, even for us believers. I often wonder if Paul had someone in mind when he was writing this particular instruction.

If you ask me, Joseph was a living testament of not repaying evil for evil, even if it took him a while to come around to forgiveness. And even though he did not grow up in the two-parent household of harmony that society celebrates today, Joseph was able to experience an abundant display of

God's favor and kindness. He was elevated from slave and prisoner to a royal officer, and he was able to use his influence to predict and prevent widespread tragedy. This brings me to one final truth about being first.

God's plans for your life are much bigger than family. Joseph's story is a reminder that the plans God made for you well in advance of placing you in the care of your family of origin are so much bigger than merely being someone's child or sibling or parent. When God took his time to knit you together in your mother's womb, he was also knitting together plans for the impact that you would have on the world. God has called you to be set apart in a world that needs every bit of the specific gifts and contributions that only you have to offer. Because we were designed to have an impact on the world and all eternity, we can confidently rest in knowing that even if our family didn't turn out to have the familial love story we'd always hoped for, our story can still turn out to be far greater than our wildest dreams and imaginations. Isn't that such a relief?

The truth is, our dreaming and discernment reveal to us only a tiny piece of a much bigger picture that God is crafting through the challenging circumstances and pathways he has called us to. This is why we must look to biblical stories like Joseph's to help build our faith. When Joseph couldn't seem to catch a good night's rest without dreaming up something wild about stars and moons, he had no idea what that would mean for his relationship with his family. He also had no idea what that would mean for Egypt. Although he and his brothers tried to put the pieces together, they failed miserably at understanding the vastness of it all. Thank God they did, or perhaps his brothers might have been even more intentional about distracting and deferring Joseph from being used so mightily. And perhaps Joseph might have been too arrogant or too fearful to use his gifts in a prison cell or in front of the royal court. Trusting that God has a much bigger plan for our lives is necessary for learning to trust our own discernment, especially when it comes to making difficult decisions or taking unfamiliar pathways that lead us to be the first.

Side Effects of Cycle Breaking

I want to take a moment to reiterate that even though we know the plans God has for our lives *are* good, that does not mean they will *feel* good. Throughout Joseph's story in Genesis, the Bible mentions that he weeps five times. He is especially emotional upon reuniting with his brothers all those years after they sold him into slavery, breaking away several times to weep alone after speaking with them. In one passage, it says that Joseph was weeping so loudly that he could be heard in the next room. Joseph was hurting.

I know this feeling all too well. I don't think there are many forms of betrayal that can compete with what you feel when you encounter betrayal from a family member or spouse. Particularly when messages from the pulpit, mass media, and our friends and loved ones consistently communicate that these are the relationships that we should be able to depend on the most. As a result, it seems that there is very little we would not do in the name of family. We make sacrifice after sacrifice, hoping to move in the direction of a picture-perfect family image, and when our efforts don't seem to be working, we are heartbroken. I've spent many nights weeping as loudly as Joseph at the mere pain of it all. Those are the moments when I have to remind myself of the truths his story reveals, including a truth that isn't so comforting: *there are side effects of being a cycle breaker.*

Joseph's story wraps up in Genesis with what feels like a biblical version of a "happily ever after." But when we turn the page to the book of Exodus, we learn that although they prospered for many years because of Joseph's obedience and favor, Jacob's descendants, the Israelites, were forced into slavery by a different Pharaoh many years later. This paves the way for another cycle breaker by the name of Moses, who, after being sacrificed by his mother out of fear for his life, goes on to become the one who is called to end the cycle of slavery for the children of Israel. Yet Moses experienced side effects of being a cycle breaker, just like Joseph before him: he was angry about the injustices his people faced, committed murder, and experienced moments of great isolation. When it came time for him to be used greatly by God, he was resistant and insecure in his abilities to do what God was calling him to do. Moses felt disqualified because of his past and his flaws, and it literally took miracles for God to convince him that he was called. But once Moses gave God his "yes," he became the first person in the Bible whom God granted the power to perform miracles of his own and was given the ability to guide the Israelites out of Egypt.

It's the side effects of cycle breaking that so often lead those of us who choose to do things differently for the first time to a therapist's couch, or a pastor's office, or a friend's dining room table. Like Joseph and Moses, before finding our way to these safe spaces, we may experience seasons of great loneliness, anxiety, depression, or moments of internal conflict and self-doubt. We may have trouble trusting the people around us who try to offer us the love we crave, or we may struggle to love ourselves in light of what we perceive as the destruction we have caused. In those safe spaces, we are reminded that these side effects are normal and, beyond that, to be expected. And we are encouraged to find our peace and strength in our "why." Being the first to do things differently or carve out a new pathway offers hope that there will be a second, and third, and fourth, and fifth, and several others after that. Choosing to chart a new path not only sets us up to be used greatly by God in this life but also paves the way for future generations who will follow our paths in the next.

The Truth about Generational Curses

By now, we've established that being set apart from your family, whether by choice or by chance, can have painful consequences. Although we can see how some stories have endings that eventually turn out to be good, not all stories end that way. When not properly attended to, the damage of darkness and sin can have a lasting impact with an expansive reach. Like most family trauma, my family story extends beyond my parents and my siblings and has had a trickle-down impact on the families we've joined with and created throughout the years.

My father's grandchildren live with the consequences of his actions. Years ago, God gave me the grace to understand that both my father and my mother were likely living with the consequences of sin from generations that came before them, passing along seeds of darkness and open doors that, until closed, would continue a vicious cycle of brokenness.

As a Black woman and a descendant of enslaved people, I've learned that many of the harmful cycles in my family have been passed on from generation to generation. I'll never forget the day a therapist shared with me how mother-child bonding in the Black community has struggled to heal from the intentional denial of bonding that existed during slavery, a practice that allowed children to be ripped from their parents at a moment's notice. As a result, it is believed that mothers who were enslaved often tried to protect themselves by not becoming attached to their children. And those children, without having properly attached to their mothers, struggled to attach to their own children. And the cycle continues.

In the church, the passing along of sin's consequences are often called *generational curses*, an Old Testament idea revealed in Exodus 20, in which God proclaims that he will punish the children for the sins of their fathers to the third and fourth generation. Time and time again in the Old Testament, we read stories of families that were greatly impacted by the sins committed by a few or even just one individual: the children of Israel were forced to wander through the wilderness for decades; tribal leaders were swallowed into the ground, leaving behind widows and children; and entire towns were burned or destroyed.

Yet, in Galatians 3, we read that through Christ the veil has been torn, and we live under a new covenant where Christ took upon the curse of punishment:

Christ redeemed us from the curse of the law
by becoming a curse for us, because it is written,
Cursed is everyone who is hung on a tree. The
purpose was that the blessing of Abraham would
come to the Gentiles by Christ Jesus, so that we
could receive the promised Spirit through faith.
(Gal. 3:13–14—emphasis in original)

As believers, we are no longer cursed, but sin does have
consequences that seep out into the lives of those around us
and create harmful cycles that need to, and can, be broken.
This is why so many institutions rightfully place a scrupulous
focus on family: in addition to serving as a foundation for how
we perceive and navigate the world, the families we are born
into undoubtedly influence what our worlds become. Research
has shown that strong family ties can provide a greater sense
of meaning and purpose, improve our well-being, and serve
as a sort of protective barrier from the stressors that we
encounter in other areas of our lives. However, the downside
of our built-in connectedness is that when our relationships
with family members are strained or unhealthy, we can suffer
severe consequences, such as increased risks for anxiety and
depression, blows to our immune system, impacts to our car-
diovascular system, and the adoption of unhealthy coping
mechanisms to deal with stress.

Prior to embracing my role as a cycle breaker, I had difficulty forging healthy friendships and relationships as I
transitioned into adulthood. Because of the secret of our
trauma, my family had been guarded and unusually code-
pendent. The lie we silently accepted was that no one could

understand what we'd been through and, of course, no one was allowed to know. I often felt isolated, misunderstood, and suspicious about the intentions of others. The consequences of my family dysfunction resulted in destructive patterns of behavior and thinking. I developed a fierce sense of independence and moved out on my own shortly after graduating from high school. I was running as fast as I could in the opposite direction of my family, eager to start a new one in the future that would right all the wrongs I had endured.

A couple of months later, I became pregnant at eighteen, following in the footsteps of both of my older sisters, who had become teen mothers in high school. My son's father and I were engaged when I gave birth, but I struggled to communicate effectively as I spiraled in doubt and insecurity about my own budding family, and we eventually broke off our engagement.

Although I had been eager to get it "right," in reality, the idea of marriage both confused and scared me, and that fear influenced my actions, beliefs, and values, outweighing what had been taught to me about families in my traditional church upbringing. I remember hearing ideas about family being preached and modeled from the pulpit but feeling that those ideas were not grounded in reality; I could not find the ideal family in existence anywhere in my life. I had always had an unshakeable faith in God, but in this specific area of my life, my fears about family life outweighed my hope. Finally, I moved hours away to another town with my son, repeating the same action as my mother to "start over" as a single parent.

That is the fundamental thing about families: until we learn how to truly trust our discernment and pursue freedom from unhealthy cycles, the patterns, values, and belief systems we gain within our family dynamics continue to repeat themselves. This is the nature of our flesh: we do what we have always done, seen, or experienced, even when we do not want to do it. And even when we want desperately to do something different.

> For I do not understand what I am doing, because
> I do not practice what I want to do, but I do what I
> hate. Now if I do what I do not want to do, I agree
> with the law that it is good. So now I am no longer
> the one doing it, but it is sin living in me. For I know
> that nothing good lives in me, that is, in my flesh. For
> the desire to do what is good is with me, but there
> is no ability to do it. For I do not do the good that I
> want to do, but I practice the evil that I do not want
> to do. Now if I do what I do not want, I am no longer
> the one that does it, but it is the sin that lives in me.
> (Rom. 7:15–20)

Can you relate? Many of us who were raised in a toxic family dynamic later find ourselves reeling as we recreate the same toxicity that caused us deep suffering. We open our mouths to talk to our children, and instead of the grace and love we so desperately desired when we were younger, we hear the harsh voice of our parents, or the curses of our abuser, or the lies we were manipulated into believing about ourselves come out instead. As the apostle Paul writes in Romans 7, this is the law of sin at work within us. Sin, even sin that is not directly our own, wages war within and around us, keeping us in bondage to its lies and destruction.

It was not until my midtwenties when I realized my story did not have to end the same way it began. This was also the time in my life when I moved away from religion and learned what it meant to have a personal relationship with Christ. Learning the true character of God and his design for our lives and our families allowed me to begin a journey to freedom that changed me forever.

DADDY ISSUES

Father to the fatherless, defender of widows—this is God, whose dwelling is holy. God places the lonely in families; he sets the prisoners free and gives them joy.
Psalm 68: 5–6 NLT

I will never forget the moment I realized I was not tied to the sins of my father for all eternity.

It was during a Wednesday night Bible study session of a women's group at a church I had just recently begun attending. A few weeks earlier, I had stumbled wide-eyed into the room, overwhelmed by the choices of small groups meeting for the night and having decided to just try one out.

The small group model was new to me; this new church held breakout Bible studies by topic or interest on the same campus one night a week, as opposed to the one-room teaching I was used to at the more traditional Black churches I had previously attended. During that old-school sort of Bible-based teaching, you were guaranteed to dive deeply into God's Word, from Old Testament to the New Testament, with a deacon in the pulpit and a handout with fill-in-the-blank questions guiding you along the way.

I love, love, love Black folks' midweek Bible study.

But I had moved to a rural, white college town for graduate school, and it had not been easy to find those types of churches. After months of traveling hours on the weekends to attend my old church back in my hometown, I decided it was time to try something new. Most of my grad school friends had been attending a much larger, multicultural church with concert-style praise and worship and a different format for Bible study, complete with the branding of "doing life together."

As a young, single mom in graduate school, I did not fit into the "double income, no kids" group, and I struggled to find childcare that would allow me to join the young adult crew who hung out on Friday and Saturday nights for fun group activities like bowling and Bible study.

The women's group seemed to be the place where I would be most likely to fit in, and quite frankly, I had grown tired of standing awkwardly in the hallway, staring at the lists of group topics while one of the campus pastors strolled to and fro, offering me a welcoming smile and asking if I needed help making a decision.

A group for women it was.

The first time I walked into the room full of women, my gut told me that perhaps this church would not work out for me after all. There was a circle full of women of all ages, but most of them were older than forty and most of them were white. I was in my early twenties and hesitant, but the women did not miss a beat when it came to welcoming me to the circle and making me feel comfortable.

During my first session with the group, the leader walked us through an activity in which we placed sand, pebbles, and rocks into a jar in such a way that demonstrated that in order for all of the items to fit inside the jar, the big rocks had to go in first, followed by the pebbles, and finally the sand. The jar was meant to illustrate how we must be sure to put God first; then the other "big" things in our lives, like family and school; and the little things that tend to zap most of our energy during the day should go in last. It was a nifty little activity, and I was grateful for the practical advice, especially as I was knee-deep in the overwhelming pressures of my graduate program. Then, we launched into a discussion and the circle shifted into a form of group therapy.

Sitting in that circle, women were open and vulnerable. They shared challenges in their marriages and with family members. They gave each other solid advice, exchanging Bible scriptures and worship songs they used to overcome the hurdles that were introduced during the discussion. They boldly submitted prayer requests for areas of their lives that I would have never dared to utter out loud. Family issues were supposed to be discussed with family only. How would their loved ones feel if they knew what these women were sharing so openly?

I am now convinced that one of the most effective schemes of Satan is to persuade us to leave God out of our most broken places, believing that we are somehow alone in a sea of picture-perfect families that picnic on Saturdays, or marriages that are never tested, or friendships that are made for television sitcoms. All too often, when we hide our secrets and trauma from others or push our truths down deep under our shame, what we are attempting to do is to hide them from God.

In the back of my mind was the huge dark cloud of family trauma, and I wondered if I could ask them to pray for me. I quickly shunned the idea with a shiver, imagining the sheer horror I would experience staring into the faces of strangers while sharing secrets that had gone unspoken and unacknowledged by my family for years. It was far too soon for me to consider speaking up. However, it was easy to see that the group was a trusted space for many of the women who chose to share. I made my observations quietly and decided to give the group another chance.

When I returned on a different night, the leader announced that we were starting a new video-based Bible study by Christine Caine called "Undaunted: Daring to Do What God Calls You to Do." She handed out a worksheet with questions and dimmed the lights. *Finally*, I thought, *a worksheet to guide our explorations of the Bible.* Hopefully, there would be less sharing and more filling in the blanks.

It was my first time participating in a video-based Bible study, and I remember feeling a tad bit judgmental as I darted my eyes around the room from woman to woman, fully engrossed in the video playing background music as a montage of Christine appeared on the screen. *This feels weird*, I thought.

But once Christine began speaking, I became completely engrossed. She told the story of how she and her brother first learned that they were adopted. A simple discovery shared in a letter had revealed that their mother and father were not who they had always believed them to be.

In this time of darkness, she said, she embraced that *facts* do not outweigh the *truth*. She quoted John 8:31–32, in which Jesus tells the disciples that if they abide in his word and hold close to his teachings, then they will really be his disciples and they will know the truth—and the truth will set them free.

In a moment when Satan could have used Christine's unshakeable love and beliefs about family to produce bondage, confusion, and doubt, she chose instead to revel in the truth she had found through the Word of God. Truth that affirmed that in the midst of her uncertain conception, she was fearfully and wonderfully made in the image of God (Ps. 139).

As the lights came back up, I wiped the tears that had slowly begin to fall down my face, and I forced my focus onto the sheet of paper in my hands. One of the discussion questions asked how the video had changed our perspectives on our relationships with our birth fathers in light of our Heavenly Father.

When it was my turn to speak, my voice trembled.

"I feel . . . free," I said, beginning to weep. And then I shared my secret out loud for the first time in a room full of strangers: "My father is an alcoholic and a pedophile."

Although my father had been absent for most of my life, his presence had been heavy. For years, I carried the weight of those labels and the actions of my father on my shoulders. I had grown to despise my last name and even some of my facial features—my face's round shape, my nose, my smile— anything about me that conveyed my connection to a man whose sinful actions caused so much pain and damage in my family. But, as Christine spoke, I felt a release as the Holy Spirit allowed her story of adoption to take root in my heart.

I am not my father.

And although my image may bear resemblance to him, I was not created in his image. I was created in the image of God. And so were you.

> So God created man in his own image, he created him in the image of God; he created them male and female. (Gen. 1:27)

That night, the women in my group introduced me to "Abba Father," an aspect of my relationship with God that was unfamiliar to me. In Romans 8:15, Paul explains that when we receive the Spirit, we are adopted to sonship and by the Spirit we cry, "Abba, Father." The Greek term used for the phrase "adopted to sonship" means that we have full legal standing as children of God. In the years that have passed since that evening when I first sat in a room full of strangers and heard Christine's powerful adoption story, I have grown to appreciate my own adoption story even more—and what it means to truly be a child of God.

Our Adoption Story

Recently, I watched a television show that focuses on a family of foster children and the challenges they experience on the path toward adoption. In one episode, one of the newly adopted foster children boasts that he has received his new birth certificate—the one with his adopted parents' names listed, instead of those of his birth parents.

As I watched him run around the house waving a piece of paper, with a smile that stretched from ear to ear, I could not help but remember the feeling I had the night when I realized what adoption meant for me. Sitting in that room with women I barely knew, I felt seen in a way that I had not experienced in as long as I could remember. Not only that, but I felt hope. After what seemed like a lifetime of dread, there was a fissure in the murky clouds of shame that had distorted what I believed about fathers and about families. What I had previously known was not all there is.

At the time, I was just beginning to grasp what it meant to be adopted to sonship, and just like the foster kid running around and proudly displaying his new birth certificate, I knew it meant that my future would be better than my past. What a revelation! When we become sons and daughters of Christ, we are issued a new birth certificate. I have full legal standing as a child of God. And so do you.

In 2 Corinthians 5:17, Paul writes, "Therefore, if anyone is in Christ, he is a new creation; the old has passed away, and see, the new has come!" In the past, I imagined this scripture to have a more specific application to things that were in my realm of control: my old behaviors, my old thoughts, my old attitudes. I would pray this verse on New Year's Eve in the hope that I would wake up on January 1 as a new creation, living a new life in a new world where I was free from my old suffering and old regrets.

Over and over and over again, I tried to will myself free from something I couldn't quite name but could feel pulling at me, no matter how hard I tried to outrun it. I had not felt free when I moved out of the home I shared with my family and into an apartment to live alone. Or when I fell in love with a man and had a child of my own. Or when I graduated from college. Or when I moved hundreds of miles away with my son to start a new life. On each occasion, it felt as if I were living a new life, but I was not a new creation. I was still the same old me, carrying my resentment and rejection from place to place.

Does any of this resonate with you? My tactics remind me of the old adage that when a woman changes her hair, she is about to change her life. In fact, I must admit I tried it once. And although the feeling was freeing, I still wasn't free. I was just the same old me with a Rihanna pixie cut. Nonetheless, our culture has normalized grandiose—and oftentimes unwise—actions as an external indicator or initiator of change. Fed up with your look? Cut off all your hair. Discontent with your daily routine? Quit your job and travel. Feeling uncertain about your purpose as you grow older? Buy a hot red sports car. If this feels like a personal attack, just know I am right there with you. In the years before I understood what it meant to be in relationship with Christ, I think I tried it all (except for the sports car). Even though we have seen how these tropes play out in the movies, we still try them anyway. And once the fleeting newness of our rash decisions wears off, we are still stuck with ourselves and the discontent that we were trying to absolve. Change may feel good, but it will never offer the same contentment of being made new.

I now know that the loophole in my annual prayer was that the newness I desired could only be found *in Christ*, not buried somewhere deep within me, or spawned by an ambitious change to my physical appearance or situational circumstances. I had somehow overlooked those two pivotal words, *in Christ*, and made "become a new creation" a personal goal, like meeting a weight-loss milestone or visiting the Seven Wonders of the World. Don't you hate when you discover that you've been misappropriating a passage of Scripture for so long?

The undergirding issues and trauma that weighed heavily upon me remained because I was placing my hope in things other than God: in my abilities, my relationships, my family, my environment, and myself. I did not understand how important it was to believe and accept what a new life truly meant and made possible for me. I simply wanted to forget the old; I did not understand what it meant to be set free from it. Unfortunately, there are not enough self-motivating mantras in the world to outrun the deep-seated trauma that some of us experience within our families or simply as a result of being born into a fallen world. Rewriting my legacy was something that only adoption could do.

When the apostle Paul writes about becoming a new creation in Christ, he is discussing a biblical concept known as *reconciliation*. In 2 Corinthians 5:18–21, Paul goes on to explain that our newness comes from God, who *reconciles* himself to us through Christ. Our reconciliation to God is a cornerstone of what is shared widely and known simply as the gospel, or the "good news." Many Christians can easily recite the premise of the gospel: Jesus died on the cross for our sins so that we may have eternal life. But in order to experience the full freedom granted to us through the gospel (and through our adoption to sonship), it is important to understand what reconciliation truly means.

Although reconciliation is often understood as an exchange or settling up of sorts, the definitions I cling to explain that to reconcile is "to make or show compatible" or "to make consistent with another." In laymen's terms, we are reconciled to God because there was an exchange that made us compatible and consistent with him. Through reconciliation, Christ became *our "old"*—God made him who had no sin to be sin *for us*—and through his death, our old passed away. Although the crucifixion was a one-time event, the impact of Christ's death extends to all humanity in perpetuity. As a result, at the moment we accept Christ and believe what he did for us on the cross, we reap the benefits of his death and resurrection and become like Christ in the eyes of God. In fact, we become co-heirs with Christ! In Colossians 1:18, Christ is described as "the firstborn from the dead." He was first, and his supremacy paved the way for our own resurrection in this life and the next. Through this process, our old died and was replaced with a newness that is eternal. And that newness is what brings us into right standing and relationship with God. But the only way reconciliation happens is in and through our faith *in Christ*. There go those two little words again.

When Paul writes to the churches at Galatia, he explains it like this: "But since that faith has come, we are no longer under a guardian, for through faith you are all sons of God in Christ Jesus" (Gal. 3:25–26). The reconciliation process was complete on the cross. Christ's death was the final step in the highly anticipated and grueling process of our adoption. When Jesus uttered the phrase "It is finished" just before taking his last breath, he was the judge signing the decree at the adoption finalization hearing.

I truly want you to get this because it took me so long to reap the benefits of this exchange in my own life. I knew the "good news," but I did not fully grasp why it was so astonishingly good. Imagine having your adoption finalized and still identifying with (and being ashamed of) your preadoption identity for years after the fact. That would be a travesty! The moment adoption clicked for me, it was like learning that my new birth certificate had been finalized and was waiting for me at the courthouse, but I had not made the time to go downtown and pick it up. This is what we do when we carry the past hurt, scandals, and brokenness of our families of origin around from place to place, instead of exchanging our old for newness in Christ.

But rest assured, our old is not limited to our relationships or experiences with the families we were born into. Our old refers to any number of issues or sins that seek to prevent us from fully embracing our freedom in Christ. Our old is the thing that invites us to question if we are truly worthy of the calling and purpose that God has placed within us. Our old is the thing that makes us want to cut our hair, quit our job, or purchase a hot red sports car. Our old is life as we knew it before Christ, and before we made time to go down to the courthouse and pick up our new birth certificate. The first step in truly getting rid of our old is to understand the exchange that was made on the cross and accept that in order to receive the full benefits of our adoption, we must make an exchange of our own: we must give God our old life and accept a new life as a co-heir of Christ. If this resonates with you, I invite you to join me in a quick prayer of acceptance:

Abba Father, thank you for the gift of reconciliation. That you would offer your son in exchange for all of my old so that I could be made new in Christ demonstrates your immeasurable love for me. For too long, I've neglected to embrace the fullness of new life that was made available to me on the cross. But now that I know, I declare that I am free from the baggage and bondage that I have carried for so long. I lay my old down at your feet in exchange for my new birth certificate. I rejoice in my adoption and give you all the glory—for while the process was finished on the cross, my new life begins now. Amen.

Before we go any farther down this path, I want you to take a moment and celebrate your adoption. Yes, I know that our adoption does not grant us a life free from suffering, but we will get to that in a moment. For now, it's time to pick up your birth certificate and run around the house with a big grin on your face. It's time to celebrate that even when you were knee-deep in your old, God knew you by name and wanted you to be made compatible with him, so he exchanged your old for Christ on the cross. That exchange—that grueling adoption process—has been completed, and you have been justified as a co-heir of Christ. It is finished. You have a new father now—and a new family, too. And whenever that old tries to bubble up inside of you, simply pull out that imaginary birth certificate and remind yourself that you have been justified through Christ and reconciled to God.

God Our Father, God Our God

Remember that fictional TV family made up of an endearing bunch of foster children? Undoubtedly, if we would have been able to follow them well beyond the adoption celebration, we would see a moment or two when friction began to rise in the new family structure. The new parents would try to establish new family traditions or guidelines, and the adopted child—in completely new territory—would struggle to adapt to all the newness, even with a heart full of gratitude for their new home and their new last name. There would be moments of tension and silence, arguments, and misunderstood intentions. I imagine that there would be plenty of tears and, then, even more gracious moments of reconciliation.

Our reconciliation to and relationship with God is no different. I wish I could tell you that the moment adoption clicked for me was followed by the voice-of-God narrator declaring: "From that day forth, she lived happily ever after as a co-heir with Christ." I imagine you would hear this voice over an image of me and the women in my small group laughing and hugging while chatting over snacks, and you would think, *Wow, what a wonderfully unattainable fairy tale!* And you would be correct.

In reality, the truth is that I struggle with fully embracing God's role as "Abba Father" in ways similar to a rebellious teenager struggling to obey and appreciate the wisdom and guidance of their parents. Chances are, you do too. Remember when I cautioned that "whenever that old tries to bubble up inside of you," you would need to remind yourself that you are a child of God? It's been my ongoing battle with *my old*—post-adoption—that allows me to write those words in wisdom. Picking up the birth certificate from the courthouse is only the beginning, and I would be remiss if I made it seem as if this were the end of our adoption story.

Just like a teenager testing the limits of their parents' love, learning to navigate the newness of being reconciled to Christ can carry its own challenges, particularly for those of us who might struggle to trust the parameters of a fully complete and safe relationship. And while most people will acknowledge that the rebellious teenager phase is completely normal, we cannot avoid the lingering impact of the years when it feels like we are at war with our caregivers or that they are somehow in cahoots, planning for our failure. Oftentimes, the enemy uses these painful growing seasons to plant seeds of doubt and rejection, and you might find yourself dwelling on questions like "Do my parents really love me?" "Why don't they want me to succeed?" "Why won't they just support me?" "Can I even believe the advice they are giving me?" "Am I a good daughter?" "Am I worthy of their love?" "Am I worthy of love at all?"

These questions may sound familiar, as it is not uncommon for us to pose similar questions to God. In fact, it often feels like the higher the tensions are during our moments of struggle, the darker the questions we ponder. In my own life, the darkness of those questions was exacerbated by my father's absence and my mother's determination for us to survive amid our dismal circumstances. Our family's survival and safety were built upon my mom's willingness to sacrifice time at home in order to pull parental double duty. As children, it can be really difficult to overcome dark and doubtful questions when it feels as if there is no one around to point you in the direction of truth. Whenever I heard others refer to God as a good father, it was difficult for me to wrap my head around what that meant for my relationship with God, because I had no model for understanding the dynamics of a good father's relationship with his child.

I have a vivid memory from my childhood that illustrates the depths of my complicated emotions regarding fatherhood. One Sunday afternoon, a couple of friends and I were gathered around the front steps leading into our church. One of the girls' father was either sick or had recently passed away—that detail is still a little murky—and another friend of mine was trying to console her. However, what is so vivid about this memory is how envious I felt. I just stood there, looking at my friend and thinking about how much better it must feel in the long run to know that your father was not with you because he was no longer alive, as opposed to feeling he was not with you because he did not want to be. At the time, I was barely a preteen and had no point of reference to understand why parents do the things they do; I just knew that my father was alive somewhere and living his life without me in it.

The pangs of that rejection and years of believing that I had a parent who did not want me sometimes made it difficult for me to accept that God had chosen me and that his choice wasn't a fluke. It also made referring to God as a father difficult for me to understand and accept. For years, I scoffed at sermons and Bible studies that echoed the question introduced on the night when I learned what adoption to sonship truly meant: What is the connection between your relationship with your birth father and your Father in heaven? Because I believed that my "adoption to sonship" had liberated me from my father's sinful legacy, I was confident that there was none.

It annoyed me that people in the pulpit hailing from seemingly perfect two-parent families would work so hard to offer this imagery to us all, especially when we did not all have fathers who were present in our lives. Another series of unsettling questions and thoughts developed in my angst: *Why does God have to be a father anyway? Why couldn't God be a mother? Why couldn't God simply be God?* My rationale argued that God couldn't be a father because fathers can leave. But then I reasoned that a mother could leave, too. In fact, as a result of our free will, any person can leave at any moment they choose. My questions were rooted in what I know about broken people and broken families. Why would anyone want God to be a father when he is so much more than that? Everything I have experienced with my father and others stands in stark contrast with the one thing I know to be true about God: he is the great I Am.

In Exodus 3, there is a powerful scene where Moses is questioning himself and debating with God about being called to lead the people of Israel out of Egypt. Moses is doubting his ability to lead effectively and believes he will need a bit more than just his word to stand on when convincing the people of Israel about his plan to escape. After a series of protests about his assignment, Moses questions: "When they ask the name of the God who sent me, what should I tell them?"

> God replied to Moses, "I AM WHO I AM. Say this to the people of Israel: I AM has sent me to you." God also said to Moses, "Say this to the people of Israel: Yahweh, the God of your ancestors—the

God of Abraham, the God of Isaac, and the God of Jacob—has sent me to you.

> This is my eternal name,
>> my name to remember for all generations.
> (Exod. 3:14–15 NLT)

This passage of Scripture offers the most significant name for God—the name that God desires to be remembered by for all generations: Yahweh. This exchange between God and Moses is the only time that God offers a name to describe himself, and he makes a point to connect his name to people: he's the God of our ancestors, of Abraham, Isaac, and Jacob. He's the God of Moses, and the Israelites, and future generations. This name is so sacred that in the Jewish tradition, it would not be spoken out loud. Instead, we find references to Adonai, Elohim, or Lord. Still, all these names fail in comparison to Yahweh, which conveys God's sovereignty, permanence, and long-standing relationship to us. He's the God of all those who came before us, and he's the God of you and me.

In Revelation 1:8, God is described as the Alpha and the Omega; the beginning and the end; the one who is, who always was, and is still to come. The sureness of God is what drew me into him. In the beginning of my walk with Christ, drawing comparisons between my relationship with God and my relationship with my father introduced a feeling of insecurity that brought out some of my deepest fears. My distorted view of relationships reasoned that God was not a man that he should lie, and God was not a father that he should leave. God was simply God; that was that on that.

Who We Are to God

A watershed moment occurred for me when, one day while discussing an in-depth study on Romans 8 with my small group, I blurted out an answer to how I knew that the Spirit was bearing witness with my spirit. The discussion stemmed from verse 16, in which, right after declaring that we have been adopted to sonship, Paul writes that "the Spirit Himself bears witness with our spirit that we are children of God" (NKJV). In other versions, "bearing witness" is replaced with phrases like "testifies and confirms" (Amplified Bible) or "joins with" (New Century Version and New Living Translation, among others). This attribute speaks to the role of the Spirit in uniting us intimately with God as his children; the presence of the Spirit in our lives is our confidence that we are reconciled to God. The question we were discussing had directed us to describe the ways we knew this to be true, and I jokingly yet confidently shared that I knew the Spirit was bearing witness for me because of the way that God knows what, and why, I need him to speak to me again and again so that I can trust him.

"I've got trust issues!" I exclaimed to my friends. "And Jesus knows that." In the time that our small group had been meeting, it became a running joke that I was the friend who needed a burning bush *and* a staff to throw on the ground in order to trust that God was speaking and I was not being tempted by my own selfish motives. However, it was also a running testimony that every time I have a question or doubt, God does, in fact, give me a burning bush *and* a staff to throw on the ground (metaphorically speaking, of course). Like Moses, I can't help but ask a couple of follow-up questions before I get started on my assignments. What started off as a moment riddled with laughter quickly became overwhelmed with emotion. In my boasting about how good God is, how well he knows me, and how the presence of the Spirit in my life offers evidence that I am, in fact, a child of God, I had stumbled upon the significance of relating to God as a child and referring to him as a father.

My own testimony had painted a picture of a God who is patient to answer each and every one of my questions, who is careful to nullify my every doubt and insecurity, and who gained my trust by never wavering in his love for me through my rebellious teenager phase. So many of us have our ability to be children and angsty teenagers taken away due to life's circumstances, and as a result of living in a world tarnished by sin. We see things and experience circumstances that force us to toughen up and rely on grit and determination to forge ahead. All the while, when we are searching for protection, wisdom, and guidance, there is no one to be found. In this way, we dupe ourselves into believing that we are our own saviors. When this happens, we forget what it means to be a child. Although I am certain this isn't the case with everyone, I am sure that those who work within the realm of adoptions can attest to seeing this sort of push-pull process play out in the lives of children who have had to fend for themselves before being placed in homes with new parents and new families. Despite how much we may pray for it, hope for it, and rejoice for it, newness can be difficult to embrace when our old is so familiar.

The question of the connection between my relationship with my birth father and my relationship with God was never about comparing God to a man (or even my father), but instead serves to reveal something about me: not having a relationship with my father influenced my ability to view myself as a daughter worthy of unconditional love, forgiveness, wisdom, guidance, protection, and everything else that a relationship with God offers. My anguish and rejection had filtered the lens I used to see myself, which subsequently affected how I related to God. I had lived a life questioning my value and expecting disappointment from others. Therefore, in ways similar to Moses, the line of questioning I often present to God is much more about my insecurities as a result of my experiences with people rather than my experiences with God. Still, God has been faithful and present to answer them all because he knows me, and he understands.

When we cry, "Abba, Father," it is this sort of intimate relationship with a sovereign God that we are invoking. This term is mentioned in the Bible only three times, and the first mention is from Jesus in the Garden of Gethsemane (Mark 14). This is the penultimate scene in his life, just moments before he's whisked away in a series of events that ultimately lead to his death. Scripture tells us that Jesus is experiencing heightened grief and anguish about his imminent betrayal and crucifixion. He's sweating so profusely with angst that his sweat is mixed with drops of blood. It's when Jesus falls to his knees to pray that he calls God "Abba, Father," and asks him to take the cup of suffering from his hands. The moment when Jesus cries out, "Abba, Father" is when the tension peaks in his story. We don't get a glimpse into Jesus's stream of consciousness in the garden, but I imagine he had some dark and doubtful thoughts. So much so that he dared to ask God to remove a cup of suffering that he knew—more than anybody— was God's ultimate will. Yet he asked anyway, trusting that

God knew him and that he understood. Jesus, encumbered by his full humanity, was appealing to God's love for him and, ultimately, God's sovereignty.

This is a poignant revelation in Scripture, when Jesus, who is God in human form, offers us another name for God. In the Old Testament, God tells us that he is to be remembered as Yahweh throughout all generations. Yet, in the New Testament, God offers Jesus as a living sacrifice to establish a new covenant and a new type of relationship with us through Christ's death and resurrection. "Abba, Father" was a name that only Jesus could use at the time, and one that we are able to use only because of what happened on the cross. While nearly a thousand names can be used to convey who God is to us, Jesus's use of "Abba, Father," depicts a father-son relationship that helps us understand who we are to God.

When the apostle Paul later explains to the church of Rome that it is because of the Spirit that we can cry out, "Abba, Father," it is a reminder that we are just like Jesus in the eyes of God. When God looks at us, he does not see the adoption papers or process; he simply sees his children. And just like the adoptive parents of children, God not only wanted us; he chose us in advance. Paul drives this point home even further in Romans 8:30:

> And having chosen them, he called them to come to him. And having called them, he gave them right standing with himself. And having given them right standing, he gave them his glory. (NLT)

As children of God, we are chosen, called, justified, and glorified—just like Jesus. Even when it can be difficult to wrap our heads around what this means, that truth still stands. I believe this is what Christine Caine meant when she explained that *facts* do not outweigh the *truth*. Being able to place our hope in Christ frees us from the cultural norms that dictate an ideal family image. Christine's confidence came from being made new *in Christ*, not from being born into a perfect family. So when her family structure was shaken, she was able to stand firm. Likewise, when you and I place our hope in our greater adoption story, it allows us to gain perspective on the purpose of our experiences within our families of origin.

The fact is that our families and relationships with people—our parents, siblings, friends, or partners—may be full of flaws and brokenness. As a result, the enemy conspires to use our experiences to taint our ability to accept that we are truly worthy of a life filled with love and freedom, no matter what our old may be. And one of the more predictable ways in which he accomplishes this is through our warped sense of what family truly means. Like adopted children who can't shake the troubles of their pre-adopted life, Satan wants to use our old to constantly taunt us with dark and doubtful questions. Fortunately, as is the case with any adoption process, our adoption to sonship did not catch our Father by surprise. He knows what we are up against, and he understands. While we may not physically have a new birth certificate to let us know that the process is finalized, it is our evolving relationship with God—evidenced by the Spirit in our lives—that gives us confidence. Even when we question the limits of reconciliation, the Spirit pursues us to remind us that our role as children of God is not by chance. We were chosen, called, justified, and glorified because God desires to be in our lives.

Once I was able to understand how significant I am in the eyes of God, I was able to put all other relationships in my life into perspective, including ones that caused deep pain and suffering. Distancing myself from the legacy of my father most likely sounds easier than it actually is. I still see the features of my father's face when I look at myself in the mirror. I still wince when I hear friends mention calling their fathers to ask for support and advice. The desire to ask God, "Why?" still resurfaces from time to time in the middle of the night. But when I consider a grief-stricken Jesus crying out, "Abba, Father," in the Garden of Gethsemane, I am reminded that God can use indescribable pain to push us forward in purpose.

WITHOUT HONOR

> *Jesus said to them, "A prophet is not*
> *without honor except in his hometown,*
> *among his relatives, and in his household."*
> **Mark 6:4**

Have you ever had someone start a conversation by asking, "Do you want to hear the good news or the bad news first?" Whenever someone asks me that, I tend to scowl at being put on the spot for what seems like an impossible choice. According to researchers, most people want to hear the bad news first so that they can end on a good note. However, an interesting finding in a subsequent study is that when people receive the good news prior to the bad news, they may be more interested in changing their behavior than preserving their mood. It turns out that being left in an unsettling mood does wonders for encouraging people to think about doing things a bit differently.

So here's the truth, family: I started with the good news. My story and your story do not have to end the same way that they began. We can choose to follow our discernment and become cycle breakers, while being confident that our newness through adoption is established in Christ and assured by God. And more importantly, we can trust that in spite of what may come as a result of the decisions or mistakes we make while walking out our faith, our standing as children of God who are chosen, called, justified, and glorified will remain.

Now, here comes the bad news: as we await our future glory, we will experience pain and suffering in this life, much of it stemming from our experiences with people we love dearly. And because many of us spend most of our formative years (and years thereafter) within some sort of family dynamic, our family members are first in line to contribute to some of our most hurtful experiences—not always intentionally, or even consciously, but with great impact nonetheless. Remember that one time your big sister would not let you play with her Barbie dolls? Or that one night when you tried to share an opinion with your mother, and she shut you down by telling you to stay out of grown folks' business?

Fleeting moments like these are most likely carved into your memory, and even if you have somehow managed to forgive and move beyond the Barbie doll betrayal of '97, the deep feelings of being hurt, mocked, isolated, or rejected may never be forgotten. After spending years in the church, I've learned that a common term for describing actions that inflict pain, suffering, or even mild discomfort upon us is *offense*. In this life, offenses come from nearly every direction: friends, romantic partners, coworkers, ministry partners, strangers on the Internet (take it from me: if you want to remain holy, never, ever read the comments), and especially our family members.

If you are anything like me (and if you are still reading, I am pretty confident that you are), you have probably heard phrases like "Turn the other cheek" or "Forgive and forget" when it comes to dealing with offense. You may have even been criticized by others for grappling with offense any longer than the offending party or your loved ones believed you should. You may have been accused of being too sensitive, overexaggerating, or callous when you took too long to make nice with someone who offended you. *It's been a week already. Are you still upset about that? Isn't it time for you to forgive?* All too often, these nudges intended to encourage us mistakenly conflate forgiveness with staying in relationship with someone who has caused you or others a great deal of harm, or acting as if the offense never occurred.

The pressure to demonstrate forgiveness through performative actions that allow others to feel better about conflict fails to register that forgiveness is an inward decision to release feelings of resentment or ill will toward a person or group who have harmed you, but not a commitment to live in harmony with them. Forgiveness is a matter of the heart, not a mechanism for attending to the guilty consciences of those who have wronged you. Remember the scripture I mentioned earlier that signaled to me that sometimes it might not be possible to live at peace with everyone? Now might be a good time to revisit that truth. In Romans 12:18 Paul writes, "If possible, as far as it depends on you, live at peace with everyone." Sometimes the nature of an offense might mean that living at peace or being in relationship with the offending party is no longer possible.

Although many offenses are minor and isolated events— the embarrassment of your mother rudely shooing you out of the kitchen for trying to contribute to grown folks' conversation—many of us may experience offenses that are major and persistent, such as a drunk father sneaking into his child's bedroom under the shield of night with cruel intentions, or an abusive loved one who routinely lashes out in anger and inflicts physical or emotional harm. Major and persistent offenses are the ones that cause irreparable damage, and the ones that are impossible to forget. Another term to describe them would be *abuse*. The path to forgiveness for these sorts of offenses is often long and rocky. The time spent in prayer seeking the grace and mercy needed to forgive someone who has harmed you in such an unimaginable way may stretch out for years or even decades. And even then, what happens on the other side of forgiveness may not look anything like what folks misconstrue forgiveness to look like; it might not look anything like being at peace.

In some families, a persistent cycle of harm that misappropriates the meaning or appearance of forgiveness can become toxic, especially when the principle moves beyond simply being a shared Christian value to becoming a form of psychological manipulation called *gaslighting*. Gaslighting is a method of mental and emotional abuse that attempts to make a person question their own memories, thoughts, feelings, or judgments. In relationships with our loved ones, this often looks like constantly being made to feel as though you are in the wrong for having a valid emotional response to offense, even when the offending person may not have truly committed to repentance or changing their behavior.

For those of us who grew up in families raised in what my pastor refers to as "scary church," even Scripture has been weaponized as a tool for spiritual gaslighting—one verse taken out of context can be preached at you in a way that causes a whirlwind of guilt and regret. You may have heard "Blessed are the peacemakers!" as an admonition to keep your mouth shut, or the popular saying "God will never put more on you than you can bear" as a means of diminishing what feels like unbearable pain. In either case, the context of Scripture is grossly mischaracterized in order to avoid confronting the messiness of conflict and painful truths.

Unfortunately, this occurs frequently in families marked by dysfunction, such as addiction and substance abuse, physical and emotional harm, or neglect. These tumultuous and sinful cycles become the shameful family secrets we try to sweep under the rug. Oftentimes, gaslighting is employed as an ineffective means of mitigating family conflict around those issues by simply refusing to acknowledge that they exist. When a family member attempts to express concern about serious offenses or painful secrets, that person is labeled as a troublemaker or an adversary to family values. In these scenarios, the end goal of gaslighting is for you to believe that the absence of conflict equals peace, even if minimizing offense means that you have to suffer in silence.

According to my therapist, this is one of the reasons why she works overtime around the holidays. For so many people, the long stretch of time bookended by taking the kids trick-or-treating in October and counting down to the new year on

December 31 is also the time when we try to contort ourselves into being at peace with offenses—minor and major—as we sit around the table with our loved ones, hoping to keep traditions alive, all in the name of family. Years ago, I was one of those people sitting in a room full of family members in the days leading up to Christmas. I had been anxious about returning home for the holidays, but then there was a moment when all the kids were playing nicely together, and my mom and sister were in the kitchen cooking with the Christmas music playing in the background, and I thought, *So this is what a "normal" holiday dinner with family feels like.*

I was finally beginning to relax when it happened. We were doing our best to secretly wrap presents at the dining-room table just out of sight of the kiddos when we realized we needed another pair of scissors. As everyone was looking high and low, a loved one—who was drunk—whipped out a machete to cut the wrapping paper. Yes, a machete. As in a twelve- to eighteen-inch-long blade on a handle that is often used like an ax . . . to cut wrapping paper. Did I mention that I was raised in the American South, where all types of folks shoot rifles, carry knives, ride horses, and enjoy all sorts of outdoor and survival activities?

Needless to say, I'm a city girl in my mind, so the machete did not sit well with me, especially with a crew of rambunctious children running around the house. I looked around and noted that a few of the other adults in the room held a look of annoyance, but I knew no one was going to speak up. And I knew what they would say if I did. *Calm down; you're overreacting. Nothing is going to happen. This is just how that person is. You know they love their knives.* But this person was drunk, and still drinking, while waving a machete around *my child*. I had to speak up. Of course, when I did, all hell broke loose, and the next thing I knew, the name-calling and yelling had begun. After being yelled at and mocked, I made the choice to get my son and leave.

A couple of weeks later, my therapist sat across from me with her mouth agape as I recounted the scene. "There was a *machete*?" she asked in utter disbelief. But even as I sat there not believing the words that came out of my own mouth, I still wondered if I had been in the wrong for making a scene, and if it was all worth disturbing the peace. Couldn't I have just endured the shenanigans for a little while, especially if everyone else was willing to look the other way? Was I not patient enough? Loving enough? Or forgiving enough to spend a couple of hours in discomfort for the sake of my family? I am betting that you are familiar with this line of internal dialogue and can relate to the feelings of guilt that go hand in hand with making the difficult decision to walk out on your loved ones. If so, then it is safe to say you have experienced some form of gaslighting.

Here's the truth: It is not okay for drunk adults to wave machetes around children or even adults, for that matter. It is not okay to have to contort yourself to sit at the dinner table at holidays with a pedophile, or someone who abuses their husband or wife, or someone who demeans or harasses you with verbal insults. And most likely, whatever the major offense was that made you consider walking away was not okay either. You and I are not irrational people (well, at least not most of the time). I know this because if anyone else in the world attempted to come near us or our children or our loved ones and put them in harm's way, we would not question our responses to these major offenses for even one second.

This is what I like to call the *stranger litmus test*. For some reason, when it comes to our loved ones and family members, we are often encouraged to minimize or accept our suffering. I cannot tell you how much it irks me to hear people say, "But that's your [insert family relation here]! You need to let it go!" as if offense committed by a parent or sibling or extended family member somehow makes the hurt more tolerable or its impact less damaging. The next time you find yourself or anyone else questioning your response to a major offense committed by a family member, pose the question: "If a stranger had committed this offense, what would my response be?" However, here's a quick note of warning: the stranger litmus test only works when we don't over-spiritualize our suffering.

I can almost hear some of you thinking right now: *I would forgive a stranger, too. It's the Christian thing to do!* Again, this is where I drive home the difference between forgiveness and forcing yourself to continue suffering as evidence of your salvation. When you forgive a stranger, or a colleague, or a friend of a friend, chances are you will establish a clear boundary around that relationship in order to protect yourself from experiencing a similar offense in the future. Unfortunately, when it comes to our loved ones, establishing such boundaries becomes a bit more difficult to do. As a result, we tend to convince ourselves that enduring major and persistent offenses—a form of abuse—committed by our loved ones is the Christian thing to do and our cross to bear on this earth.

As believers, oftentimes our experiences with spiritual gaslighting can result in a warped understanding of our relationship to pain and suffering. This misunderstanding finds footing in a seemingly standard Christian belief that we should bring our offenses to God; we are taught that we should pray for strength to forgive and lead with love, extending the same mercy and grace to others that God did for us when he exchanged his Son for our sins. We were wretched sinners, after all, and God loved us so much that even in our darkest moments he made a way for us to be brought into right standing with him. Surely, the least we can do as Christians, or even simply as good people, is to try to model this love to others—especially those who have wronged us. This is a principle embedded in the Lord's Prayer, a meditation that many of us cling to when we experience hardship. "Forgive us our trespasses, as we forgive those who trespass against us" becomes a mantra for dealing with offense. Regrettably, in our attempts to be like Christ, we sometimes lose perspective.

Instead of our acknowledging that pain and suffering was never a part of God's original plan for our lives but was introduced as a result of the original sin, suffering can somehow become a standard by which we demarcate our sanctification. Many of us take the apostle Paul's instruction in Romans 5 to "rejoice in our sufferings" as a newfangled litmus test of our own, whereby the extent to which we are able to suffer in silence (or in love, as some characterize it) is interpreted as proof of our sanctification. We hold onto the image of Jesus sweating drops of blood while praying in the Garden of Gethsemane or wearing a crown of thorns on the cross, preparing to fulfill his purpose, and dignify the Christian life as one that should be marked by pain and humiliation. In some of the worst-case scenarios, we even make idols of our trauma. We tell ourselves,

"Look at how much abuse I can endure; surely this proves that I am like Christ." But no matter how much we endure, we cannot out-suffer Christ, whose pain and humiliation settled a debt that we could never repay.

Here's the thing about our suffering: much of what the apostle Paul preaches about suffering is with regard to being persecuted *for Christ*, in the same way that Christ suffered *for us*. In fact, in Romans 8:17, Paul explains that sharing in suffering is a part of our reconciliation and a caveat of being co-heirs with Christ. According to Paul, this suffering occurs so that we may share in the glory of Christ, not in the glory of ourselves. There is no award in heaven for the Christian who endures the most, and we are no less Christians when we protect ourselves from needless suffering. And before you ask, yes, there is such a thing. Peter explains it like this:

> If you're abused because of Christ, count yourself fortunate. It's the Spirit of God and his glory in you that brought you to the notice of others. If they're on you because you broke the law or disturbed the peace, that's a different matter. But if it's because you're a Christian, don't give it a second thought. Be proud of the distinguished status reflected in that name! (1 Pet. 4:14–16 *The Message*)

We suffer as Christians because we live in a world plagued by sin and set in opposition to Christ. Yet Peter indicates here that there is suffering that we can, and should, avoid. In other words, there is suffering for Christ and then there is suffering for different matters. Those different matters—murder, theft, evildoing, meddling, and so forth—do not glorify God. Can

God give us the grace to endure needless suffering? Yes. Can he use every bit of our pain and suffering for good? Yes. But God does not delight in our suffering, and neither should we. I want you to read this next sentence out loud with me: God does not desire for me to live a life of pain and suffering.

Time and again, Scriptures tell us quite the contrary. In Jeremiah 29:11, we are encouraged that God has plans to prosper us, not to harm us. In John 10:10, we are reminded that it is the thief who comes to kill and destroy, but Jesus came so that we may have life and have it abundantly. In order to live an abundant life, we must know when it is time to separate ourselves from needless suffering. When you feel yourself being tempted to make an idol of your trauma, here's another question to consider: Does my suffering glorify Christ?

If the harm being done to you is not for Christ's sake, then you can be confident in your decision to walk away, even if it means walking away from a family dinner or a relationship with a loved one, and even if it breaks your heart to do so. I would be lying if I told you that this would be easy, because it's not. The hours upon hours I've spent on my therapist's couch clutching a tear-stained tissue is proof that the pain of self-preservation can be horrendous. But unlike the needless suffering that stems from different matters, the pain of separation in pursuit of the abundant life God has planned for us has purpose. The pain of separation from needless suffering is honorable.

At What Cost?

You know, it was never my intention to become one of those "my therapist says" types of people. In fact, when I started going to therapy sessions while in graduate school nearly a decade ago, I was very resistant to the idea that some outside person could help me make sense of my family trauma. It had been almost three years since I hightailed it out of my hometown on the hunt for greener pastures. I had been living in a small, rural college town while I completed my master's degree and had decided to stick around to pursue my doctorate. During the first year of my doctoral program, two significant events made an impact on my family dynamic: my son's father got married and my mom moved in with me temporarily.

Did you just wince? I hope so, because that would let me know that you understand just how challenging and lonely this period of time was for me. I was pursuing my dream of education while feeling that my dream of happily ever after was slipping from my grip. At the same time, after years of living on my own as an adult and single parent, I was once again coming home to my mother. And you and I both know, no matter how old you are, some mothers still . . . mother. After being caught one too many times sobbing in my room by my mom—and without being able to articulate the wide range of feelings that had brought me to tears—I decided to take advantage of the five free sessions offered by the University Health Center. I think it's safe to say I was feeling overwhelmed.

When I walked into my first scheduled session, I was almost defeated at how different my therapist and I appeared to be. I was a young, Black, single mom in graduate school. She was an older, White, lesbian woman with years of experience in her profession. I was grappling with my faith and what it meant to have a relationship with God, while some of my most significant relationships were teetering on the brink of implosion. Understandably, I had no idea where she was in life personally, but she made no mention of religion or spirituality. When she asked what had brought me in, I mumbled that it was a combination of my mom moving in, not fitting in with my family, and feeling lonely. Her eyes lit up, and she pressed me for more details. It turns out that family troubles are a universal language, especially for the graduate and professional students who she worked with constantly—exactly the types of people who tend to be cycle breakers.

Over the next five sessions, it felt as if we were running circles around what had really brought me in, until I ultimately admitted it: I did not want to be living with my mother. But I could not—would not—ask her to leave. There was no way I was doing that! It was absolutely impossible, out of the question, and unreasonable to think that I could ask my mother to move out. The five free sessions ended, and we continued meeting at the student discounted rate. She continued to validate my emotions while questioning my position on the issue, and I kept resisting the notion of setting boundaries with my mother.

"Listen," I told her one day, "I'm Black! Which means that I can't turn my back on my mama! It is what it is." For weeks, I would leave our sessions all worked up at the audacity of that woman suggesting that I, the youngest of my mother's four children, attempt to stand up for myself. At the time, of course, I did not realize that my resistance was the result of the childhood trauma, spiritual gaslighting, and distorted sense of duty toward family that I had observed in my family, and others, while growing up.

Finally, one day I broke down and explained to her that what I meant by blurting out "I'm Black!" was that my mom had sacrificed too much for our family—and me, especially—for me to ask her to leave. In addition to the treacherous terrain that Black parents navigate raising Black children, my mother had experienced an unimaginable betrayal at the hands of my father, survived a divorce, worked two and three jobs at a time, navigated losing our family home, prayed, fasted, sacrificed, and more, all for us kids. Although my childhood and our relationship had been far from picture-perfect, I knew that my mother had done the best she could do, and then some, to pave the way for me to be on that very campus as a first-generation student. The least I could do, I felt, was suck it up and get a grip on the anxiety and depression that was threatening to overtake me.

"At what cost?" she asked me. "And how does this arrangement play out in the end?" I was stunned. That question rocked my world. At the rate I was going, I did not want to follow where the answer to that question was leading me. I was struggling in my classes and not performing well at my graduate assistantship. My son, who was just starting school, was witnessing arguments and tension that he had never seen before in our home. In order to avoid conflict, I simply sulked around my apartment in silence, brimming with the resentment of feeling powerless in my own home. I was so wound up that I was experiencing physical symptoms of anxiety, including chest pains, insomnia, and loss of appetite. "At what cost?" was the question that led me to realize that I needed separation from my suffering more than I needed the validation of offering myself and my home as a form of selfless sacrifice.

I wish I could tell you that I navigated the end of our living arrangement with ease, but that wouldn't be true. That chapter was one of the most difficult chapters in the story of my relationship with my mother, and when she left, I did not immediately exhale a sigh of relief. But I continued going to therapy, and I continued to seek God for peace with our circumstances. Eventually, I found myself enjoying a much greater sense of peace and clarity on the other side of our separation than I had felt since long before. Today, I think my mom would candidly agree that our relationship works so much better when we are not living under the same roof.

Still, even now, I share that story with apprehension of the gravity of "talking bad" about my mother because I'm still a Black girl, and Black folks still don't take lightly to kids "bad-mouthin' they mamas." Anyone who has witnessed an epic "Yo mama" diss gone awry on school grounds can attest to that. But the reality is, as we grow older, so many people struggle to make sense of the feelings and emotional responses that we have toward our parents or family members, especially those that can be perceived as a lack of love and gratitude. When I had questions about navigating my family's circumstances, I felt that there were very few places I could go, and my sessions on the couch with my first therapist started me down a path of extending the same grace and sense of protection to myself that I had extended to my family members and the image of our family for most of my life. Although my therapist did not identify as spiritual or religious, I can testify that she was doing the Lord's work. So many therapists do.

Years later, I was at a mountaintop retreat for professional Black women when I realized just how common strained mother-daughter relationships are among my peers. A simple loving-kindness meditation turned into a nearly hour-long session of tear-stained tissues in a room full of women suffering in their relationships with their mothers. As one of the women openly sobbed across the room while recounting the impact that her unhealthy relationship with her mom was having on her mental and physical health, I sat in dismay, silently remembering the question "At what cost?"

What Would Jesus Do?

The inevitability of pain and suffering is our bad news. However, making the decision to separate ourselves from needless suffering is a choice that we can decide to make. At the root of my transformation into one of those "my therapist says" types of people is my desire to unabashedly and transparently share with you that if you are facing the difficult dilemma of confronting a relationship with a loved one or family member that is a source of needless pain and suffering, you are not alone. I don't know that just because of what I learned in therapy; I know because when I was battling with my own decisions, God revealed this truth to me in his Word. If my story is not enough to convince you that separation can be honorable, we can turn to the Bible for the story of another person who had to make the difficult decision to walk away from his family: Jesus.

In Mark 6:1–6, we learn about the rejection Jesus faced in his hometown and from his relatives. Just prior to his return to Nazareth, Jesus had completed a streak of miracles: he drove a legion of demons out of a man into a large herd of pigs and into the sea, where they drowned; he healed the woman with the issue of blood; and he raised a girl from the dead. Then, he set off to return to his hometown, along with his disciples. Upon his arrival, he began teaching in the synagogue, and at first, many who heard him were amazed. But then something shifted among the onlookers, many of whom were related to Jesus and had known him long before he became a great rabbi who performed miracles. Their amazement gave way to doubt, and they began to question his wisdom and power. In Mark 6:3, the Bible says that they were offended by him. In response, Jesus tells them,

> A prophet is not without honor except in his home-
> town, among his relatives, and in his household.
> (Mark 6:4)

Scripture tells us that Jesus could not perform any miracles there, with the exception of laying hands on a few sick people and healing them. He was amazed at the unbelief of the people of Nazareth, and so he left to continue his work in other villages. Yes, *Jesus* left.

I don't know about you, but the image of a stunned Jesus walking away from his relatives and the place where he was raised resonates deeply with me. We don't know much about Jesus's childhood, beyond the fact that he stayed behind for three days on a family trip to Jerusalem, hanging out with teachers in a temple, but we do know that Nazareth is the place where he became strong in his spirit, increased in wisdom and stature, and found favor with God and men. If we lean into the humanity of Christ, we might even imagine that he was looking forward to returning home with his disciples and excited about what he might accomplish among his family and friends. Then came the offense.

In this story, we learn that offense is often a double-edged sword. Sometimes the conflict we experience may not be the result of major or persistent offenses committed against us; it might be that our mere existence offends others. When Jesus returned to Nazareth, he was not subjected to an obvious abuse or major offense, but he was still able to acknowledge that remaining in the presence of those who were unable to support him would be a hindrance. Even when offenses are simple or slight, they may still warrant separation. Whether you are the offender or the offended, Jesus's choice to walk away in order to fulfill his purpose elsewhere offers guidance for considering what conditions might need to be met in order for us to do the same.

Are you being subjected to undue scrutiny? Although they were originally amazed by his wisdom and power, the people of Nazareth quickly began to scrutinize those very same attributes of Jesus. How did he get to be so wise? Hadn't he grown up in the same place and under the same circumstances as they had? Why wasn't he as ordinary as everyone else? Their determination to paint Jesus as being "just like them" revealed their lack of belief and hope in their hearts. Like Jesus, many of us encounter naysayers who, because they cannot imagine or fathom some of our God-given traits and abilities, simply dupe themselves into believing the worst about us. However, like the people of Nazareth, those who subject others to undue scrutiny reveal much more about themselves through their questions than could ever be revealed about us in our answers or actions.

It wasn't as if Jesus was not used to being questioned—his disciples were a walking FAQ page, and so many of his encounters with ordinary people were marked by questions about his ability and identity. But these questions were asked in amazement and hope by people who wanted to believe that their Savior had come. The experience of Jesus in his hometown illustrates the difference between those who ask, "Who do you think you are?" and those who genuinely want to know more about you. In his one-sentence response to the people of Nazareth, Jesus demonstrates that he understood the difference between the two. It is impossible to satisfy questions that are meant to diminish. Knowing this, it becomes easier to reconcile our decision to reject the scrutiny of destructive spectators by simply walking away.

Are those around you offended by your obedience? Jesus was sent to fulfill a mission, and from the moment he left his parents at the age of twelve to hang out in the temple, he made it clear that he was about his father's business. He had a laser-sharp focus on what needed to be done to fulfill his purpose, and that included demonstrating to those around him through his profound wisdom and power that he was the Messiah. In other words, when Jesus arrived in Nazareth and began teaching, he was simply being obedient to the will of God for his life. The reaction of his relatives reveals how sometimes our obedience can ruffle feathers among those who are not privy to our calling. Radical obedience among ordinary believers can appear irrational, irresponsible, and inconsiderate. Unlike Jesus, whose calling fulfilled widely known and foretold prophecies, the prophetic and spiritual unctions we receive are not easy to convey to those around us, especially if we don't have the full understanding ourselves—which we rarely do.

When we obey strong and spiritual nudges to do things like drop out of college, end an engagement with our dream partner, give away all of our belongings, or move abroad to live the life of a missionary, there is a good chance that those decisions will be met with strong reactions from our loved ones. However, there is a difference between those around you not understanding your obedience to God and being offended by it. Once again, we can reference the lack of understanding the disciples expressed time and again while following Jesus. Although the disciples had questions and expressed concerns about the actions of Jesus, they were never offended by them. When others are deeply troubled by your willingness to step out in faith and do what you know you are being called to do, it may be time to take a step back and evaluate the status of your relationship with them.

Is the fulfillment of your purpose being stalled? Perhaps one of the most jarring revelations about the rejection of Jesus in Nazareth is that he could not perform any miracles in his hometown. This is especially remarkable, given that in just a few scenes prior, the woman with the issue of blood had been healed by simply touching the hem of Jesus's garment as he was walking, making his way through a crowd. In that moment, her faith was so strong that it placed her in a position to receive a miracle. Jesus was literally a walking source of wonder-working power, but the unbelief he faced in Nazareth was so severe that he could not have the same impact on relatives in his hometown that he had made on strangers in towns prior.

In the same way, the fulfillment of our purpose can be limited by the people who we are in relationship with. When we are surrounded by others who lack hope and faith—or people who scrutinize, doubt, and undermine the hope and faith we possess ourselves—it can do much more than hurt our feelings; it can hurt our potential. As humans, we naturally respond to the emotions and behaviors of those around us. When our friends and family members believe in our potential, it is easier to find the will to silence the quiet voice of fear and doubt. However, when we are bombarded with the negative emotions and thoughts of others, our fears and doubts can evolve into paralyzing agents of prevention. The fact that Jesus could not perform miracles in his hometown illustrates how being in an unsupportive environment for a moment too long can thwart the plans that God has for our lives. Are the negative people in your life worth sacrificing your God-given purpose?

Whenever I find myself struggling with the difficulty of walking away from a toxic relationship or environment, I revisit the story of Jesus in Nazareth and consider what would have happened if he had remained among his relatives in spite of the scrutiny, offense, and rejection he encountered there. I reflect on what that might have cost him—or us. This consideration captures the sentiment of my therapist all those years ago, when she encouraged me to weigh the cost of my failure to establish boundaries with my mother. It also echoes the teachings of Jesus to weigh the cost of being a disciple. In Luke 14, Jesus told a large crowd of followers,

> If anyone comes to me and does not hate his own
> father and mother, wife and children, brothers and
> sisters—yes, and even his own life—he cannot be my
> disciple. Whoever does not bear his own cross and

come after me cannot be my disciple. For which of you, wanting to build a tower, doesn't first sit down and calculate the cost to see if he has enough to complete it? (Luke 14:26–28)

When we set our minds to be disciples of Christ, there will be collateral damage. There are crosses to bear and conflicts to endure, but we stay the course because of the hope we have in Christ. As Jesus details a comprehensive list of people and possessions that the crowd must hate in order to follow him, he is really offering a forewarning of how people and possessions can come between us and the calling God has on our lives.

When our love for people and possessions outweighs our love for God, we can find ourselves at odds with our purpose. It should serve as no surprise, then, that Jesus chooses to include family members as the litmus test by which he asks those in the crowd to evaluate their commitment to following him. These are the people whom we love dearly, and it is because of how much we love them that we often imagine ourselves beholden to the manipulation, abuse, or rejection we may experience in relationship with them. But if we truly desire to be like Christ, then we must be bold enough to remove ourselves from circumstances where needless suffering endures and where we find ourselves living without honor. On the other side of that decision, we enjoy the fulfillment of our mission and our ministry, unencumbered by the disappointment or discontent of those around us, and empowered by the possibility of achieving our God-given potential.

MY GOD WILL RESCUE

> *But the salvation of the righteous is from the LORD;*
> *He is their strength in the time of trouble. And the*
> *LORD shall help them and deliver them; He shall*
> *deliver them from the wicked, and save them,*
> *because they trust in him.*
>
> **Psalm 37:39–40 NKJV**

The story of Jesus at Nazareth demonstrates that we can choose to walk away from needless suffering and scrutiny at the hands of our relatives. But beyond the fierce love and loyalty we hold for our family members, there may be other less honorable reasons why we struggle with making this difficult decision. If we are being honest with one another, we can admit that one of the reasons we often stay in relationship with those who harm us is that we believe we can save them.

We look at ourselves and our own redemption story and want so badly for others to experience the newness we have in Christ, and the freedom we gain when our old things pass away, that we tell ourselves that we cannot walk away from the relationship until some sort of transformation has occurred. Oftentimes, we try to combat the scrutiny from others determined to prove that we are "just like them" with counter appeals and sweeping actions to convince them that they are "just like us." Ultimately, we want to bring others along with us, regardless of whether or not they are up for the task.

After all, beyond simply being a redemptive quality, setting out to "save" others is the Christian thing to do. So much so that in the New Testament, the apostle Paul tells the church at Corinth that he would do pretty much anything to win souls for Christ. He'd make himself a slave, or become a Jew, or live as one under the law, or become weak, or do just about anything else for anyone if it meant that he could save them (1 Cor. 9:19–22).

It is easy to read those words and find ourselves similarly compelled to go out and do great things for the kingdom—and especially for our loved ones. If Paul is willing to go to such lengths for strangers, must not we be willing to go to the ends of the earth in order to see our family members saved? After all, Scripture tells us that anyone who does not provide for their family or household has denied the faith and is worse than an unbeliever (1 Tim. 5:8). Our interactions with our family members are our most prominent opportunities to be, as they say, the hands and feet of Jesus. And that is an opportunity we should not take lightly.

Consequently, it makes perfect sense that when we look up and see our family members in trouble, we attempt to do all we can in order to see their circumstances changed. And it is easy to understand that we simply do not feel accomplished until our efforts are effective. But we are called to be disciples—not saviors. Paul was not preaching that we should start shape-shifting and going to the end of the world simply because we feel it is the right thing to do, and he was not suggesting that we seek to save others in order to prove our value. Instead, Paul makes it profoundly clear that he was not preaching for personal glory; he was preaching for the gospel, and to share in the blessings of doing so (1 Cor. 9:23). This is a difference between being a "good person" and being a disciple. And this is the type of "saving" that brings comfort and hope to our souls.

These next few pages require absolute honesty, so I am going to start by telling you the truth: this chapter unmasks the lies we tell ourselves about our desire to be heroes. It asks us to get real about the things we do to feel good about ourselves and the things we do for the glory of God. It involves unpacking some of the ugliest and darkest sources of our need to be victors, those that go even to the extent of compromising the calling God has placed on our lives. It reveals that in addition to wrongly believing that we are designed to suffer, many of us buy into the idea that we are designed to be saviors. And it exposes this type of "saving" as one that wreaks havoc in our lives and chips away at the hope we claim to profess.

Simply put, our heroic efforts are sufficient only when done for the glory of God. With an honest heart check, we can determine when our attempts to rescue others are being fueled by false motives. And with an evaluation of our mental, emotional, and spiritual wellness, we can be alerted to the potentially hazardous outcomes of our human striving. Quite frankly, trying to single-handedly rescue those we care about can be grueling and back-breaking work. When we attempt to pull others out of dark and undesirable circumstances by our own might, we can unwittingly enter an unproductive game of tug-of-war where no one wins in the end.

Unfortunately, that does not keep us from trying. This is because the longing to declare victory over the darkest of circumstances appeals to our sense of pride. While the desire of our hearts may be to see our loved ones rescued from their circumstances, it is our pride's desire to see ourselves as their rescuers. It is easy to understand how this could become a slippery slope for believers, who take great pleasure in being overcomers. After all, it does feel really good to win battles against the enemy.

Very little compares to the joy we experience when we are able to see the hand of God at work in the lives of our loved ones, especially if we can later testify that we had anything to do with it. If it had not been for us, we tell ourselves, beaming with pride, our loved ones would have never given up alcohol, or started going to church, or found that new job, or turned their lives around, or . . . While our ability to be used by God to perform miracles in the lives of others is fundamental to our faith, the harmful truth about our desire to be saviors is this: when we boast about our ability to make a difference in the lives of our loved ones, we flirt with the danger of believing that the victories we are able to witness belong to us, instead of God alone.

The Hero in Our Story

At the root of our pride is the desire to make people proud. When you are the first in your family to do things differently, the need to not disappoint can be especially poignant, particularly if you have already ruffled some feathers along the way. So when the opportunity comes along to lend a helping hand or show up in a crisis, it can be really easy to want to be the one who saves the day. Pride is really sneaky in that it creeps up within us even when we are sincerely trying to do good for others. We start off by simply wanting to see a victory, and then, before we know it, our focus has shifted to needing to be the victor.

In the Old Testament, we see this steady progression of pride play out in the story of King Saul, whose struggle with insecurity and the cultural pressures of being the first king of Israel ultimately limited his ability to make the lasting impact he so desperately longed for (1 Sam. 8–15). After years of receiving guidance from a host of judges, Scripture tells us that the people of Israel wanted to fall in line with surrounding nations and appoint a king to lead over them. Although their request rejected the established role of Yahweh as their king, God listened, and the Lord led Samuel to anoint Saul as their king. However, from the very beginning of his story, we see Saul struggle with insecurity and scrutiny—two common facets of the cycle-breaker experience. We experience insecurity because we have been called to do things that no one has ever done before, along with scrutiny because everyone has an opinion about how those things should be done—while wondering if we are the right ones to do them.

Shortly after Saul was anointed king, he was given the opportunity to make the Israelites proud and put his naysayers to shame by rescuing the city of Jabesh. While preparing to head into battle against the Ammonites, Scripture tells us that "the spirit of God came powerfully upon" Saul (1 Sam. 11:6 NIV), and he led Israel to victory over their enemies. After this win, Saul declared "the LORD has rescued Israel" (v. 13 NIV), and he went on to be confirmed king in the presence of the Lord.

Although Saul continued to reign over Israel for forty-two years and won victories wherever he turned, it was during his battle against the Philistines that his pride began to burn. In the midst of the intense battle, Samuel had given instructions to Saul to remain at Gilgal and wait for him for a period of seven days. However, when the seven days were up, Samuel had not yet arrived. At the time, the Israelites were hard-pressed, and Saul's men had begun to scatter. Feeling the pressure to secure a victory, Saul made arrangements to offer up a burnt offering to the Lord in order to seek his favor.

On the surface, it seems as if Saul was doing the right thing by seeking the Lord in a time of crisis, but his actions went against the law, which required that he wait for a priest. Furthermore, he went directly against the instructions of Samuel, which were to wait for his arrival. Immediately after making his offering, Samuel arrived and rebuked Saul because of his disobedience. Later on, in a battle against the Amalekites, Saul once again defied the instructions of the Lord given to him by Samuel. For this battle, he was instructed to completely demolish the Amalekites, but instead he spared the king and the best of the sheep and cattle.

The next day, he was so pleased with his victory that he went off to build a monument to himself. At this point, Saul's pride is a raging fire. When Samuel finally catches up with Saul, his rebuke is a harrowing revelation of the Lord's regret for making Saul the king and an admonition against his growing pride and idolatry:

> Samuel continued, "Although you once considered yourself unimportant, haven't you become the leader of the tribes of Israel? The LORD anointed you king over Israel." (1 Sam. 15:17)

It is important to note that Samuel was heartbroken over the Lord's rejection of Saul. Scripture tells us that after the Lord spoke to Samuel regarding his regret, he wept all night. When he finally has the opportunity to confront Saul, he reminds him of his previous feelings of insignificance when set up against the power of God, and then he reminds him that it was only by God that he was anointed to become king. In spite of his greatest efforts to warn the people of Israel against establishing a monarchy, Samuel is devastated to witness Israel's first king become a cautionary tale. Israel did not just want a king; they wanted a hero. And Saul had foolishly attempted to rise to the occasion, without preserving his dependence upon God.

I imagine that Samuel was speaking to Saul with tears in his eyes, emotional and hoping that he would see the error of pride at work in his life. He knew that it was only through full surrender that Saul and the people of Israel would find favor with God. Sadly, Saul had demonstrated that his desire for favor among people was greater than his desire to find favor with God. And even though Saul sought to acknowledge the

Lord through continued sacrifices, Samuel candidly explained to Saul that God desires obedience and surrender more than sacrifice. As Saul began to realize the gravity of his disobedience, he pled for Samuel to help maintain his reputation by honoring him in front of the elders and people of Israel.

Whenever I revisit the story of Saul, I am reminded of just how easy it is to lose sight of the importance of complete surrender and obedience to God, especially when we are tempted by the allure of winning. Not only do we want to win battles; we also want to win favor among people. In general, neither of these desires is wrong. Of course we want to be liked by the people we care about. But when our motives move away from pleasing God to pleasing people, we can end up disappointing the one who matters most. I don't know about you, but I cannot imagine a world where I have to live with knowing that the Lord regrets choosing me. My heart shudders at the mere thought.

This beckons us to stop and reflect on the battles we are currently fighting. Are you trying to secure a victory on your own or with the help of God? Are you willing to stand still and wait for God to show up? Or are you forging ahead because you feel pressured to do the right thing in front of others? Saul let his desire to please people take center stage, even as he sought to keep God in the peripheries of the audience. He was doing the "right" things, but for the wrong reason: to glorify himself and win the approval of the people of Israel. What his actions failed to acknowledge is that God had already approved him when he set him apart as king, and that was all the approval he needed.

Like Saul, so many cycle breakers initially step out in faith only to fall prey to a new cycle steeped in pride. We refuse to

walk away from potentially harmful and hope-crushing relationships because we want to make others proud. Receiving
approval and applause from people who used to doubt us
can be intoxicating, and we find ourselves seizing any opportunity to remain a hero in their eyes. We see the red flags
in our relationships—the abuse of persistent harm, undue
scrutiny, unwarranted offense, and stalled purpose—but we
stick around because we want to be the ones who finally get
through. Instead of trusting that God will bring his work to
completion with or without us, we want to be able to proclaim
that we made a difference. But sometimes we forget that it was
only by the grace of God that we are in a position of influence
in the first place. And even if we are moderately successful on
our own, our efforts will never compare to the victories that
could have been won with God as the hero in our story.

If Not Me, Then Who?

Although pride can start off with a simple swell in our chest, it
often gives way to its more menacing cousin: idolatry. When
we buy into the lie that it is our personal mission to win battles
for our loved ones, we can find ourselves teetering dangerously
on the edge of idolizing ourselves and acting as if it is not God's
power that does the rescuing. For evidence, see Saul's decision
to build a monument to himself after the battle against the
Amalekites (1 Sam. 15:12). Or perhaps you might consider my
own story as a more modern cautionary tale.

I learned the dangers of having such a God complex early
on in my adult life. You may be vaguely familiar with the use of
this term to refer to people with the common personality flaws
of being addicted to power and believing themselves to have

way more influence in the lives of others than is actually the case. My journey to adopting such an inflated view of myself began when I was only eighteen years old and God blessed me with the means to provide for myself financially.

After a rigorous application process, I was one of one thousand prospective college students selected as a Gates Millennium Scholar (GMS), an award that came with a scholarship covering my full college tuition, guaranteed for up to ten years. Because my family had grown up with less than enough, this scholarship was a big freaking deal. I will never forget the Sunday afternoon when my mom and I shared our testimony with the church that my college education would be 100 percent paid for. We stood at the mic with a shout of joy, whooped and hollered through tears, and then took off running around the church to the beat of tambourines. It was amazing. To this day, being a GMS scholarship recipient is one of the greatest testimonies of my life, and a testament to God's grace and mercy when I needed it the most. What I did not realize as I was rejoicing was how receiving what we believe we need the most can reveal what is lacking in our hearts.

At the beginning of my first semester in college, the scholarship fund mailed me a refund check for more than $5,000. This was the amount that was left over *after* paying my tuition and fees for my first term in school. I was ecstatic. But more importantly, I was rich. If that made you chuckle, count your blessings. In the aftermath of my parent's divorce, my family rarely experienced financial circumstances that left us with an excess of thousands of dollars. Although we never lived on the streets, we did experience seasons when we went without a home and lived with family members and friends. Whenever we were settled in a home, it was evident that our household was of the paycheck-to-paycheck variety. Our lights were on and hot meals were always on the table, but there were enough financial woes to prevent us from being able to afford luxuries like frequent restaurant dining, family vacations, or college tuition. Before I took the check to the bank, I made a copy of it on a Xerox machine to honor the magnitude of the miracle. I still have the paper copy of that first check to this day.

The first thing I did with the money was to pay my tithes. Of course, after whooping and hollering all around the church, I certainly had to honor God through my tithes and offering. Next, I bought myself a reliable pre-owned car to get back and forth from campus. I was over the moon when I was able to pay for it in cash. I had already used the award letter to secure an apartment for my sister and me, and I made sure to put some cash to the side for my portion of the rent over the next few months. The best thing about the $5,000 refund check was that it was only the first in a series of refunds I would receive every semester as a GMS scholar. The steady stream of scholarship income meant that I was one step closer to something my family had never experienced: financial freedom.

Once I had all of my necessities taken care of, I did what I imagine any other well-to-do person would do: I started looking out for my family. Over the next couple of years, I used the money from my scholarship refund checks to cover the necessities for some of my loved ones, like household utilities, clothing, and food. I chipped in for upscale dining experiences and family outings. I helped buy my mom a car. I even paid a loved one's bail to get them out of the county jail. If there was an opportunity to share the blessing of finally having more than enough, I never hesitated to offer to chip in—even if no one had asked for my help. Am I starting to sound a bit like King Saul?

Whenever I was able to assist with a family crisis, I would tell myself that the feeling of pride I experienced was simply gratitude that God had allowed me to sweep in and save the day. What I did not realize at the time, however, was that I was building a cycle in which I would continually swoop in with the proverbial "S" on my chest in an attempt to rescue my loved ones, and then sit back and enjoy the praise of being the one person whom everyone could depend on. By the time I moved away for graduate school, I had fallen in love with the field of journalism, an area of study that was ineligible for the final five years of GMS funding. After years of riding on a financial high, I rolled into my new town with a few thousand dollars in my savings account and the arrogance of someone who had not needed to worry about finances for four whole years.

I was dead broke within months. The "S" on my chest now stood for "super-broke." I was so broke that I would order large pizzas on Tuesdays with a $5 coupon and eat leftover pizza for dinner for the rest of the week. When I got tired of pizza, I would get the cheapest pack of hot dogs and hot dog buns, with a big bag of chips, and have the same lunch and dinner for days. I was miserable. Looking back, I can admit that perhaps what pained me the most was no longer being able to fulfill my role as the self-ordained family rescuer. To make matters worse, I falsely began to believe that if I could not help myself, there was no way I could be of value to anyone else.

In addition to the damage that going broke did to my self-esteem, I grew resentful that after four years of playing superhero for others, no one was in a position to rescue me. The anger that I experienced when others were not able to do for me as I had done for them should have been my first indicator that my heart posture was one of pride and idolatry, not of grace, mercy, and sacrifice, as I had tried to convince myself (and others). The expectations that we have when we do for others give witness to our motives. My feelings of resentment lasted longer than I care to admit. When I regained some semblance of stability, I went right back into rescue mode, captivated by the idea that I was proving my value by making a difference. Only this time I had raging resentment in tow.

Inviting my mother to live with me during the first year of my doctoral program was the denouement of my season of playing savior. Out of all of my family members, demonstrating to her that I could take the title of provider was perhaps the most tempting appeal to my ego. Being able to provide for one's parents is often seen as a pinnacle of adulthood; I was prepared to do so in my early twenties and as the youngest of her four children. Now *that* was worthy of a round of applause—or so I believed. Regrettably, the season finale came with a hard-fought lesson of what happens when we try to take the place of Christ in our personal recovery missions.

When my mother moved out, I had to confront the difficult emotions that came along with such a monumental failed mission, and why I had been willing to risk my own physical and emotional health to maintain an ideal of what it meant to "save" everyone around me. What I discovered was that somehow along the way, I had adopted a mind-set of "If not me, then who?" If I did not step up to the plate, no one would. In hindsight, it is easy to see that I had become a first responder of sorts, and by doing so, I was moving away from full surrender and total trust in God. It pains me to consider how many times I encouraged my family members to call on me, while making no mention of God. Although I was not a king leading an army of troops in the fight for our nation, I was fully engaged in the same internal battle that King Saul waged—the desire to be the hero in my family's story.

Can you relate? I certainly hope so, or else I run the risk of sounding completely full of myself right now. But we agreed to be honest with each other at the beginning of this chapter, and it is only through our honesty about these challenging truths that we'll be able to pursue freedom in this arena of pride. I know so many people who proudly carry the badge of being the one who makes things happen in their families that it is easy to overlook the issues of idolatry, insecurity, and identity that can plague the lives of cycle breakers. Like Saul, we may be trying to do the right things, but with the wrong motives. And this is why we struggle to walk away from even the most disastrous circumstances: our pride does not want us to believe that our loved ones will be okay without us.

I am almost ashamed to admit that it took only four years of being in a position to offer some financial reprieve and influence for me to buy into the lie that it was my calling to be the one—and perhaps the only one—to save my family from all the messy, painful, and heavy darkness that had been plaguing us for years and perhaps even generations. The fallacy in my thinking was exposed when I went broke and new crises emerged. Instead of surrendering my family's circumstances to God through prayer and fasting, I had convinced myself that in order to remain a change agent, all I needed to do was figure out how to make more money. What had started off with a shout of praise to God had evolved into the root of my God complex: money had become an idol.

The thing is, it is really easy to make an idol out of the things we lack. King Saul is a perfect example of this. When Samuel tells Saul that he is to be the future of Israel, Saul's response is that his family is the smallest and the least important among all of the clans of the Benjaminite tribe (1 Sam. 9:21). When Saul gets a taste of what it feels like to be the most important man in Israel, he completely loses sight of the importance of being obedient to God in his role as king. In my family, we grew up without money, so when I found myself with just a few thousand dollars in my bank account, I got a taste of what it felt like to be the savior in our story. Along the way, I lost sight of the importance of trusting God to do the saving. As a result, when my family's trauma continued to come to a head, I stuck around trying to secure a victory, even at times when I should have taken a step back and allowed God to do what only God could do.

While we are busy breaking cycles, we cannot ignore that pride and idolatry often visit us hand in hand. We make idols out of anything we put our trust in before Jesus, and especially when we cling to a version of ourselves as the victor in our stories. But at the end of the day, anything we cling to more than God is an idol. Perhaps in your family you have seen idols made of other things, such as quality time, feelings of love and acceptance, professional influence, or even respect. Once we can attain or offer something that has been lacking for those around us, it is easy to use our blessing as a means to barter for validation and to satisfy our sense of pride.

Are we still being honest here? If so, take note if any of these "I" statements resonate with you:

- I am the only one who has the free time to do homework with the kids after school. If it were not for me, they would be failing miserably.
- I am the only one with a lasting marriage in this family. If they do not heed my advice, their marriage probably won't last.
- I am the only one with high-profile contacts and experience in the business world. How would anyone else in this family get a decent-paying job if it were not for me checking their résumés and putting in a good word?

By convincing ourselves that we are the only ones who can meet the needs of our loved ones, we set ourselves against impossible standards that contribute to the needless suffering and offense that deep down we desperately want to separate ourselves from. Only, in this scenario, the pain and anguish we experience are a direct result of our own pride.

The bad (but oh-so-relatable) news here is that so many people fall into similar thought traps. We have seen the role of the rescuer play out in testimonies, news broadcasts, and primetime television time and again. A family or group of friends are down on their luck when, suddenly, one person makes it big. As they rise to the top, that person manages to bring everyone they care about along with them. The proud mom beams on the red carpet. The supportive sister shines from the sideline. The distant cousin becomes the loyal assistant. The mega-mansion becomes a family compound, and everyone gets keys to new cars in the semicircle driveway. The big shot is loved and adored by everyone around. The family lives happily ever after, and none of the trauma and turmoil they endured before one person's big break ever resurfaces again. Whew, the fairy tales we believe.

In fact, much of what our culture teaches us about preserving and providing for our family rests upon the notion that we must stick together. When one person wins, we all win. And while the idea of a life where we and all our loved ones win is nice, this notion leads us to inadvertently hold tightly to the inverse: when not everyone is winning, we wrongly believe that somehow we have all failed. When we find ourselves in family dynamics where not everyone is winning or moving forward on the same page, many of us struggle to accept the various and distinct journeys that our loved ones are on, and some of us take the failures of our family members to be a reflection of our value. In this scenario, we falsely accept responsibility for the actions and consequences of others because of how much we love them—even when their circumstances are beyond our control.

I want to take a moment right now to speak directly to you, letting you know that the battle your loved one is facing is not your fault. To believe that it is, is to fall prey to the schemes of Satan, who wants us to imagine that there is something we could have done or should have done to single-handedly intervene or influence the conditions of the lived experiences of our loved ones. When we browbeat ourselves into believing that if we just tried a little bit harder, we would be able to rescue our loved ones, we inch closer into the realm of pride and idolatry. Putting the onus of someone else's circumstances squarely on our backs would suggest that we do not trust God enough to intervene by any other means than by sending us as a savior. If you often grapple with the question "If not me, then who?" then I have a replacement mantra for you: "If not me, then God."

I simply cannot stress how tough of a lesson this was for me to learn. Up until the moment when I drained my bank account in graduate school, I had falsely believed that my scholarship had rescued me, and that money and stability would rescue my family from our troubles. Therefore, when I finally hit a wall in my finances, it felt as if every wall around me was tumbling down. When I was faced with the difficult dilemma of taking a step back in my relationship with my mother, I realized that there were some things that money could not rescue me from. More importantly, I finally accepted that I could not rescue everyone—or, for that matter, anyone—around me. Only God can do that.

> Because he has his heart set on me,
> I will deliver him;
> I will protect him because he knows my name.
> When he calls out to me, I will answer him;
> I will be with him in trouble.
> I will rescue him and give him honor.
> I will satisfy him with a long life
> and show him my salvation. (Ps. 91:14–16)

So far, I have been tiptoeing around this truth, but I think it's time to make it plain: God may use you to perform someone else's miracle, but he does not need you.

God is our Deliverer.

God is our Protector.

God is our Rescuer.

God is our Savior.

And we must trust that God can be all those things to our loved ones. It may be hard to believe this, but God loves the people you love even more than you love them, and his plans for them are much bigger and better than anything you could ever imagine. On top of it all, God can accomplish the plans that he has for our loved ones without subjecting us to needless suffering or circumstances that chip away at our hope.

After my mother moved out of my home, I sat back and witnessed God perform miracle after miracle in her life—none of which required my help. And to think I had the audacity to believe that she was better off with me, even when our living arrangement was wreaking havoc on us both. For once, it was time for me to take a hard look at myself in the mirror and ask, "Who do I think I am?" The truth is that I cannot be a savior when I myself am in need of salvation. As I have gotten older, my prayer has consistently been that God remains the hero in my story. After all, rescue missions fare much better in God's hands than in mine. And unlike God, I have come to appreciate that I am finite and there is always a limit to what I can do.

Are You a Family First Responder?

Do you know any first responders? These are the people who are specifically trained to be first on the scene of an emergency situation. People like EMTs, firefighters, paramedics, or police officers, who go through rigorous training to gain the skills needed to tend to medical or other emergencies while additional help is on the way. Oftentimes, we celebrate our first responders as hometown heroes who fulfill what is perhaps the most significant role in saving the lives of so many. Without the assistance of a first responder, many of the miraculous testimonies we share about the people we love would never come to fruition. If you know someone who occupies this role, they most likely take great pride in the emergency rescue work that they do. Yet there is a chance that when they speak about their day-to-day experiences on the job, they might hesitate to share the severity of the toll that their work takes on them.

The life of a first responder is marked by traumatic experiences. Day in and day out, they arrive first on the scene to circumstances that you and I could probably never imagine. Chaos and confusion, tragedy and danger all go hand in hand with their job description, and they are expected to perform their role without giving in to the weight of what surrounds them. It should be no surprise, then, that many first responders also suffer from secondary trauma themselves, and some may even develop post-traumatic stress disorder (PTSD).

Researchers indicate that roughly 30 percent of first responders develop behavioral health conditions, such as depression, stress, and suicidal ideation. This is in comparison to a rate of 20 percent among the general population. These statistics reveal the undeniable impact of repeated exposure to trauma. Yet, even with stakes this high, first responders answer the call because risking one's life to save the life of someone else is one of the most notable and honorable actions one can take.

This is the mindset that many of us possess when we step into the role of first responders in our own families, especially when our families are plagued by dark secrets and harmful cycles. I would characterize a "family first responder" as some-one who routinely intervenes in family crises with the intent to rescue others; this is not just a one-time thing. This describes those of us who have had to leave home in the middle of the night to search the streets for our loved ones struggling with addiction, time and time again.

Children who have had to parent their parents or who have never felt safe enough to call on their parents in a time of need.

Siblings who face blows while standing in the middle of the physical altercations of their loved ones.

People whose stomachs drop when they see a certain family member's name flash across their phone.

Like a firefighter running into a house set ablaze, we are willing to run into the fire if we believe we can save the life of someone we love. Day in and day out, we find ourselves responding to scenarios that are mentally and emotionally draining at best, and physically challenging and dangerous at worst. Miraculously, we perform heroic actions without any training or qualification, beyond leading in love. Surely God's grace covers us whenever we face the fire set by our family members.

That being said, the mental health consequences that first responders face make it clear: there is only so much that one person can take when it comes to witnessing some of life's most daunting circumstances. I imagine that a part of what makes it so difficult to step away from the role of a first responder is that once you arrive on the scene of your very first crisis, you begin to realize how broken the world is. Then, day after day, you are exposed to even more brokenness, and it becomes more and more difficult to spend your days doing anything other than responding to cries for help.

As believers, we are also compelled to tend to the brokenness of the world and the brokenness of our loved ones. But just as an orderly society depends on first responders to tend to those who are broken, we have a first responder of our own: Jesus. In fact, he's already offered up his first response to all the world's brokenness: his body on the cross. Now, I am by no means trying to minimize the importance of lending a helping hand to our loved ones who are in need, but I am encouraging you to consider if you have allowed God to show up to the crisis before you arrive.

It may seem backward to say that God is the first responder, as opposed to the doctors or other emergency care providers who perform heart surgery or life-saving procedures in the end. But this is precisely the role of God in our lives: he orchestrates the makings of miracles. He brings the right people to the right place at the right time. He gives the spiritual nudges we need to provide what's lacking in the lives of others. He imparts wisdom and knowledge into our spirits so that we know exactly what to do in times of crisis—and exactly when to do it. When we try to step into this role, our lack of qualifications is brazenly exposed.

So, how do we know if we have haphazardly stepped into the role of being a family first responder? We know by the extent of the post-secondary trauma in our lives. Consider the following questions:

- Do you feel hopeless about your family's circumstances? ("There's no way they will ever change . . .")

- Do you sometimes think bad thoughts about your loved ones? ("I wish they would just leave me alone, go away, or . . .")
- Do you sometimes have negative thoughts about the significance of your own life because of your familial circumstances? ("I will never amount to anything because of where I come from . . .")
- Do you consume drugs or alcohol or entertain other vices as a means of escaping the reality of your familial circumstances? ("If I just have a drink or two, it will be easier to . . .")
- Do you sometimes go days at a time in a state of overwhelming sadness because of your thoughts about family? ("It's hard for me to be happy, knowing the crisis that my family is facing . . .")
- Do you struggle to be at peace around other families or around people who have the qualities you wished your family members possessed?
- Do you often feel as if no one else could ever understand what you are going through with your family?

If you answered "yes" to a couple of these, there is a good chance that you, my friend, are ignoring the red flags in your recovery missions and approaching burnout, if you are not already there. If I have not convinced you already, now might be a good time to schedule a visit with your therapist. Or find one if you don't have one. Just saying. I know how difficult it can be to accept that trying to help the people we love the most is causing us to suffer and crushing our hope. Remember, it took me months of therapy to be honest with myself. And it has probably taken you months, or years, of trying to rescue others to reach the end of your rope. But here's the thing—as believers, we are called to be the salt of the earth and the light of the world (Matt. 5:13–16). Who are we truly helping when our rescue efforts cause us to lose our saltiness and hinder our ability to shine?

I told you at the beginning of this chapter that things were going to get real, and perhaps a bit ugly. And here we are.

The good news about dark and ugly things is that God can make them beautiful. He wants to release us from our darkness, comfort us in our mourning, give us a crown of beauty for our ashes, and adorn us with a garment of praise for our despair (Isa. 61). But that's only if we let him. Some of us hold onto our loved ones so tightly that letting go seems unimaginable. If this is the dilemma that you are currently facing, take heart in knowing that God's grace is sufficient for even the darkest and most grim circumstances that we face, and our familial circumstances are no exception to this truth.

You don't have to be the hero.

You don't have to make anyone proud.

You don't have to be the strong one.

You can admit that you're human.

You can rejoice in your weakness.

You can rest knowing that when you take a step back, God can step in and perform miracles.

FALLING OUT

> *Cast your burden on the LORD,*
> *and he will sustain you;*
> *he will never allow the righteous to be shaken.*
> Psalm 55:22

If you are a "sciencey" person like me, you have probably heard of Newton's third law: for every action, there is an equal and opposite reaction. In spite of the fact that many people do not have a strong grasp of what this actually means, or if it is even true, this scientific law is so widely recited that many are familiar with it even without knowing Newton's first name. I mean, honestly, do you remember it? I went through almost a full page of online search results before I was able to track it down. It's Isaac, by the way. Isaac Newton's third law of motion.

Okay, now—back to the science.

If you have heard of Newton's third law of motion, you most likely finished reading the previous chapter with one question on your mind: What happens next?

What happens after I realize that my desire to rescue my family has been fueled by the wrong motives, or has led to harmful emotional and spiritual outcomes? What happens when I reach the end of my rope and relinquish my first-responder status? What happens when I truly surrender my familial circumstances to God and take a step back?

The truth is, I don't know. Your family circumstances are so unique that anything could happen. Your decision to step back or stand up for yourself could be the catalyst for a loved one to experience their Saul-to-Paul conversion that allows them to finally be able to see the impact that their behaviors, attitudes, or beliefs have had on you and others (Acts 9). Or your boldness could agitate something within them that causes them to lash out against you in anger or hurt. For some, reconciliation or restoration of a relationship may be a possibility within weeks. Yet others may feel compelled to pursue absolute estrangement for several years, or forever, depending on the severity of your circumstances.

Regardless of where you fall on this continuum, your action will most likely trigger a reaction. And if you are more of a Scripture person than a science person, you don't have to take Newton's word for it—just read a chapter or two of Proverbs. That book of wisdom is chock full of verses that basically say that if you do this one thing, then this other thing is likely to occur. I use the word "likely," because although it contains an endless source of godly wisdom, the practical tips included in the book of Proverbs are not guaranteed. However, they do offer some helpful insight into the art of living.

In the same way, I cannot offer you definitive answers to your questions about what happens next, but I can offer some general reactions you may need to prepare for in the event that you find yourself facing the difficult predicament of life on the other side of falling out with your family.

For starters, you can prepare for emotional whiplash, or the emotional and spiritual responses that you experience in the aftermath of a traumatic event. Next, you might want to prepare for the backlash, or the responses you get from your loved ones once you decide to establish boundaries or hang up your first responder uniform. Unfortunately, you will also need to prepare for the gasps from outsiders, who struggle to hide their contempt of your decision to be bold enough to take the unconventional step of distancing yourself from your loved ones. And, finally, you can look forward to a response from God, whose grace and mercy are sufficient for whatever decision you choose to make.

Whiplash

At approximately 3:23 a.m. on January 1, 2020, I was in the front passenger seat of a car with my mother, sister, and nephew, headed eastbound on I-10 in Houston, Texas, when I heard a loud bang. Before I could mentally process what was happening, I heard the screaming prayers of my older sister, who was in the back seat of the car with her son. We were heading to drop her off at a bus station when a drunk driver slammed into the far-left tail end of my mom's car, causing us to spin out, untouched, on the otherwise empty highway.

The spinning and screaming stretched on for seconds that seemed like hours before I realized that we were headed straight for a wall. I didn't scream. And unlike what they say on TV, I didn't see my life flash in front of my eyes. Instead, I remember thinking how absolutely horrible it was that we were blindsided on a Houston highway, which was one of my mom's greatest fears. And then I braced for impact.

We hit the concrete wall in such a way that the far-right front end of the vehicle was at an almost perfect forty-five-degree angle, forcing the car to stop gracefully right as my door was being pushed flush up against the wall. Immediately, I switched into rescue mode and jumped out of the window, hopped over the wall, and pulled my nephew out of the back seat. Once my mother and sister were safely out of the vehicle, I went back to cut off the engine and grab our phones to call for help.

All in all, the fact that we were able to walk away from that accident was a complete miracle. At the hospital, I remember staring at a clock on the wall while waiting for results from all our tests: CT scans, X-rays, MRIs, drug tests, you name it. We were put through the wringer for hours before being cleared to head home just in time for shift change. While completing the discharge paperwork, the doctors were confident that we had sustained no major injuries, but they warned us to be prepared for the whiplash.

We were sent home with a cocktail of painkillers and muscle relaxers, but outside of being a little bruised and shaken up, I felt fine. We even made a little detour to IHOP for a quick family breakfast before heading home to deal with the aftermath of having a car totaled in the wee hours of the first day of the year. When we finally settled down at home, I looked over the recommended dosage of my prescription and huffed. I could not believe they had so easily handed out this slew of narcotics; there was no way that I was going to be an active participant in this country's opioid crisis. I took a couple of over-the-counter ibuprofens instead and went to bed.

On January 2, 2020, my body realized that it had been flung and spun around while being held down by a seat belt the day before. The pain was excruciating.

The achiness ran all through my body, as if I had been in the gym with a team of bodybuilders, or in the ring with a boatload of boxers. The light bruising from the day before had darkened to a seat-belt-sized lash across my chest. My back burned and my neck was stiff, and all I wanted to do was figure out a way to numb the pain.

This was the whiplash.

If you have ever been in a major car accident, you know that the true extent of your injuries is often not revealed until days, sometimes weeks, later. It is almost as if the trauma occurs so swiftly that it takes a while for your muscles and nerve endings to connect with your brain and accept that something awful has occurred. Then, once all the parts of your body finally get together on the same page, you get an official response: excruciating pain.

For me, the fallout from family blowups or offenses often follows a similar pattern. One moment, you are cruising through life, and the next, you are slammed into by the thing you never saw coming: the controlling behavior, the impenetrable pride, the physical or sexual abuse, the pangs of greed. In the moment of the crisis, you may experience extreme clarity regarding what must be done. You remove yourself from the situation. Maybe you call for help (therapists or pastors). You evaluate the damage and determine that you have done all that you could do. You take a step back and go your separate ways. And then one day, perhaps several days or weeks later, you wake up and find yourself in unbearable pain.

The truth is, even when it is absolutely necessary, establishing boundaries or distance between you and your loved ones can feel almost as devastating as the physical and emotional wounds we suffer when we remain in toxic relationships. In the days and weeks after my accident, I kept wondering which was worse: getting slammed into by a drunk driver or recovering from the hit. Whenever the doctors and lawyers asked me how I was feeling, all I could think was, *I am feeling like I wish this had never happened to me.* If you have ever experienced one of those things that you could never see coming, inflicted upon you at the hands of a loved one or family member, I am sure you can relate.

"Why me?" or "I wish this had never happened" can become recurring thoughts in the aftermath of deciding to take a step back from the people we love the most and the people who our culture tells us should love us just the same. Trying to navigate the world without the built-in support structure of your family of origin can be immensely difficult, especially if you are attempting to do so for the very first time. Just like the aftermath of a horrific car accident, even if you walk away feeling okay, you can expect to find yourself longing for the sense of connectedness or structure that you experienced before your relationships took a turn for the worst. This is the whiplash.

By no means am I intending to feed into fear. Don't question yourself—getting slammed into by the thing you never saw coming is not your fault. You were not in control of what happened to you. But you *are* in control of how you deal with the aftermath. And there are good ways and bad ways to pursue comfort and healing.

Underestimating the impact of the fallout can leave us vulnerable to even more unnecessary suffering. Take it from the person who shunned the doctor's advice about how to lessen the pain that was sure to come: it is much better to prepare yourself than to wait around and see how bad the impact will be. Otherwise, you might find yourself waking up one day staring at the thing you know is not any good for you but hoping that it will help take away your suffering.

Like most addictions, opioid dependency often begins with someone in unbearable pain. In the beginning, opioids offer relief from suffering and give the person in pain the chance to relax. Initially, the drug works by attaching to receptors in the body to block pain signals, while encouraging the body to release dopamine—our "feel-good hormone"—instead. In this way, opioids literally operate as a buffer that prevents your body from grappling with the full weight of pain. However, over time, it is not uncommon for the pain-relieving effects to decrease. Then, not only does the original pain return, but its arrival comes hand in hand with a dangerous dependency.

If we are not watchful, the things we do to deal with the emotional fallout from family dysfunction can operate in a similar fashion. Once the whiplash kicks in, we may cling to passions, people, or patterns that offer temporary comfort but can ultimately contribute to other, more hurtful problems in the end. One pattern I recognized in my own life is that whenever I was suffering from emotional whiplash, I found myself turning to unhealthy relationships with men that did not honor God. The story of the girl chasing after guys because of her "daddy issues" may sound like a cliché, but the idea would not be so overdone if it did not have a grain of truth. Although, of course, I never called it that.

It was actually my mother who named it for me. One morning she called me early to pray with me against what she felt was a spirit of loneliness that was trying to overtake me. In the days prior, I had fled a family holiday meetup held at her home that had resulted in arguing and chaos. In a world of frustration, I stormed out of the house with my son and drove three hours on Thanksgiving Day to get away from the drama. Not wanting to spend the holiday alone, I had allowed a guy who had been pursuing me to come spend the night. When my mother called me the next morning, I was lying listlessly in bed, feeling practically numb. I knew I had made a huge mistake, and the precision of her prayer on the other end of the phone confirmed it.

"This is not you, baby girl," she told me. "This is a spirit of loneliness."

After we hung up, I began to weep. Up until that point, I had not been able to name my feelings of loneliness and rejection; I just knew that I felt like something was missing. Whenever things blew up and I chose to take a step back from my family, I would reach out to men in order to chase a feeling of connectedness and belonging, even as fleeting and fruitless as those moments were.

The verbal assaults and conflicts I have experienced at the hands of my loved ones could often feel like venom had been spewed at me. That type of emotional pain is punitive and suffocating—it feels as if the air is being pressed out of your lungs. As a result, I would run to the first place I felt I could breathe. But even though the flings would offer a temporary buffer from the pain, over time those pain-relieving tactics would weaken in strength and I would be left lying listlessly in bed, reeling from the agonizing absence of belonging and the ghost of regret.

This pattern of deceitful coping continued until the season of my life when I joined the small group that eventually led me to pursue true freedom. Through my relationships with those women, and my growing relationship with God, I discovered that the enemy was using my family conflict to work up feelings in me that would invite me to open doors that were extremely difficult to shut. Satan is sneaky in that way. Scripture tells us that we should remain alert because our enemy lurks around like a lion, waiting for the opportunity to devour us (1 Pet. 5:7–9). When we are in the throes of whiplash, we are in a state of vulnerability, and those are the times when we need to cling to God the most.

As my spiritual foundation grew stronger, I began to notice how my ways of coping with family conflict were chipping away at the peace and hope that I craved. It became clear that the whiplash from my persistent emotional wounds was driving me to a dependency on unhealthy methods of connection. Furthermore, the guilt, shame, and regret I felt as a result of my poor coping mechanisms would leave me feeling separated from God, in addition to being separated from my family. I was operating in dysfunction on top of dysfunction, until I asked God to help me break this pattern's stronghold on my life.

One year, I took my petitions to God while participating in my church's annual Daniel Fast, a twenty-one-day corporate fast based on the testimony found in Daniel 10:12–13. Most churches participate in the fast at the beginning of the year in order to become more sensitive to God's voice, increase in wisdom, and gain clarity in vision. I was tired of the back-and-forth of whiplash and emotional dependency on unhealthy connections, and I was desperate for God to intervene in my circumstances. When I started the fast, I was in a relationship with a man who had served as the equivalent of soul food in my life for two years running. One minute he was my comfort, and the next he was my misery. By the time the fast was finished, so were we. The only way I can explain comes directly from Scripture:

> Then the disciples came to Jesus privately and said, "Why could we not cast it out?" So Jesus said to them, "Because of your unbelief; for assuredly, I say to you, if you have faith as a mustard seed, you will say to this mountain, 'Move from here to there,' and it will move; and nothing will be impossible for you. However, this kind does not go out except by prayer and fasting." (Matt. 17:19–21 NKJV)

In this story, the disciples had just witnessed Jesus heal a boy who suffered from a pattern of dangerous seizures. On their own, the disciples had not been able to heal him, and they wanted to know why their efforts had not worked. Jesus responds by telling them that some healing simply requires prayer and fasting.

It was through prayer and fasting that I was able to identify my harmful pattern of coping with emotional whiplash, and it was also through prayer and fasting that I was able to break the pattern completely. Once I was able to process the falling-out with my family without a crutch, I was able to find healthy ways to fulfill my cravings for connectedness, structure, and belonging. For example, I continued to practice vulnerability with members of my small group at church, and I spoke with my therapist about ways to cultivate deep and fulfilling relationships with people outside my family. (Trust me—we will revisit those later.) By intentionally establishing a support system in my life to prepare me for the things I never could have seen coming, I learned that on the other side of whiplash, I could enjoy a healthy distance from hurtful relationships with a clear mind and a hopeful heart.

In the end, my new healthier pain-preventing strategies taught me how to quickly and safely recover from emotional whiplash moving forward. In fact, it reminds me of the advice the doctor gave me as we were discharging from the hospital on the day of that dreadful accident: "Trust me," he said. "You are going to want to take these prescriptions before you need them."

Now it's your turn. Can you identify the pain-relieving patterns you use to cope with emotional whiplash? Instead of pursuing unhealthy romantic relationships, maybe you find yourself overeating. Or perhaps in order to avoid the stillness of being alone, you spend your time overworking. Maybe you do not think you have a pattern at all, but in reality, you press pause on your ministry and spend time wallowing in shame and regret. Maybe you have taken up the nasty habit of gossiping about other people's families to mask the discontent you feel within your own. Whatever the case, identifying the pattern helps us surrender our weaknesses to Christ and remain alert to our vulnerabilities.

Backlash

While emotional whiplash could be considered a standard personal reaction to a fallout with your loved ones, the responses you receive from your family members may be a bit more unpredictable. In fact, it could be easier to imagine a pharmaceutical commercial in which the narrator describes the life you could have with a groundbreaking new treatment, only to speed through the long list of side effects at the end. Indeed, good things can come from establishing distance from your family, but you run the risk of experiencing one or more pretty awful reactions. Unfortunately, there is no way to predict which ones might occur.

The silent treatment. Gossip. Gaslighting. Ridicule. Lashing out in rage. Harassing messages or phone calls. Withholding favor or provision. The list of ways you might experience backlash from a fallout with family members seems endless. And with every adverse reaction, the threat of a new wound emerges. Oftentimes, it is the long list of possible side effects that keeps people who desperately need medical intervention paralyzed by fear. In the same way, many of us find it hard to contend with the potential outcomes of upsetting the people we love the most. Fortunately, unlike the latest groundbreaking medical treatment, we can place absolute confidence in our full surrender to God because we serve a God whose mercies never fail.

Because of the LORD's faithful love
we do not perish,
for his mercies never end.
They are new every morning;
great is your faithfulness!
I say, "The LORD is my portion,
therefore I will put my hope in him." (Lam. 3:22–24)

When we reach the ends of our rope, taking a step back forces us to wait on the Lord. Sometimes distance is needed for God to complete a work in our family members, and at other times, this space allows a work to be completed in us. Whatever the case, while we wait, we can trust that we won't be consumed by backlash. But that does not mean that we won't feel its impact.

You may have gathered by now that I am not completely estranged from my entire family. I speak to some of my relatives routinely, while contact with others is rare. Then there are some with whom I experience what I would describe as seasons of estrangement, characterized by periods of time when we enjoy closeness, followed by phases when we appreciate some time apart. These sorts of estrangement patterns—separation from one family member but not all, or separation cycles—are actually more common than you might think. In fact, some researchers estimate that family estrangement among certain groups in the United States, such as college students, may be almost as common as divorce. And just like divorce, the shockwaves of separation are experienced and, oftentimes, expressed by all involved.

You can probably imagine that when my mother and I were at odds and chose to go our separate ways, things got a bit tense between my siblings and me. As the youngest of my mother's four children, you better believe that my older siblings had an opinion or two about my decision. The interdependence of familial relationships often presents like a domino effect: sometimes you can't remove one without knocking all the others down. After suffering the regret of my failed recovery mission in graduate school, I realized that if I desired to maintain some semblance of connectedness with my loved ones, I would need to establish some boundaries. Especially if I wanted to remain connected while maintaining my mental, emotional, and spiritual stability.

In recent years, *boundaries* has gained ground as a sort of self-help buzzword. Trust me, this observation doesn't just stem from my fascination with self-help hashtags on social media or my many years on the therapy couch; boundaries are kind of a big deal. And it's probably because they work. In fact, I could hardly believe when I was introduced to the work of Dr. Henry Cloud and Dr. John Townsend, two psychologists and authors who have teamed up to write not just one but several books that emphasize a principle that was certainly never instilled in me when I was growing up: boundaries are biblical.

While growing up and going to church in the South, it felt as though only elders were given the benefit of boundaries, while the rest of us were fair game. In turn, there were a slew of people in your life—including your parents, pastors, teachers, church mothers, and deacons—who could comment on your physical appearance, force you into hugs, plant sloppy kisses on your cheeks, and even snatch you up if you were perceived to be getting out of line. Raising any objection to their behavior was likely to be seen as a sign of disrespect, not self-preservation. And disrespecting elders would absolutely not be tolerated. Sadly enough, I know this cultural code is not limited to Southern Black church life.

As I look back, it pains me to consider that so many of us were indoctrinated with the fear of backlash when we felt the natural inclination to stand up for ourselves, up until the point that we settled on silence instead of physical and emotional safety. But consider the advice that Paul gives to Titus about doing what is good as a leader in the church:

> Do not get involved in foolish discussions about spiritual pedigrees or in quarrels and fights about obedience to Jewish laws. These things are useless and a waste of time. If people are causing divisions among you, give a first and second warning. After that, have nothing more to do with them. (Titus 3:9–10 NLT)

Although Paul is instructing Titus on how to address people who are causing division in the church, his advice offers a master class in boundary setting. Here, Paul reveals that grace is in our warning, but wisdom is in knowing when to draw a line and enforce it. At some point, we have to be able to establish what is acceptable and unacceptable behavior from the people we are in fellowship with. And that is exactly what a boundary is. In the same way that we would shun foolish quarrels and confrontations from people who attempt to wreak havoc in the church, we should also do the same for those who desire to wreak havoc in our personal lives.

Unfortunately, establishing boundaries almost always opens us up to receiving backlash, especially when they are enforced in familial relationships that our culture tells us have no bounds. Thankfully, we have already established various litmus tests to affirm that—no matter which codes our culture espouses—there are some offenses and behaviors that we simply do not have to endure. So what do we do when we know that drawing a line in the sand might threaten the established (and often dysfunctional) order of things? We teach a master class in grace.

Grace can be understood in two ways: extending love and mercy to those who have not earned it, or withholding fair consequences from those who may deserve them. After a fallout with family, this could look like being the first person to reach out and try to make amends when the time is right, or choosing to not respond in anger when on the receiving end of accusations or malice. If a relationship has tension, you might find simple ways to continue honoring a loved one while maintaining your distance, such as sending flowers or "thinking of you" cards on holidays and birthdays. By doing this, we can affirm to our loved ones that establishing a boundary does not mean we are withholding our love. Just as Christ demonstrated his love for us before we were reconciled with him, so too can we demonstrate our love for others before they make things right with us.

But sometimes, grace can also mean simply allowing the distance to remain and preserving the peace for everyone involved. This could look like having separate holiday celebrations or avoiding scenarios where your personal boundaries may result in feelings of resentment or discomfort among others. Grace could mean leaving some phone calls unanswered and some messages unreturned. This kind of grace requires humility, patience, wisdom, and restraint. And this is the type of grace that distinguishes needless suffering from suffering for the glory of God. Enduring offense that crushes your hope and robs you of your peace is far different from enduring offense so that your hope and peace may be preserved and shared with others.

Finally, our master class in grace also requires that we extend grace to ourselves. Grace for the times when we do not get our responses right. Grace for the times when we falsely believed that it was our personal responsibility to right a wrong. Grace for the times when the backlash gets under our skin and we reflect back the offense that has been hurled at us. Grace that allows us to forgive ourselves as frequently as we forgive others. If I am being honest with you, this is the kind of grace I have had to extend to myself far too many times. And most likely, you will too. Because falling out with your family can be absolutely heartrending, and it reveals when our surrender is anything less than complete. While we wait for the Lord to complete the work he has begun in our lives and in the lives of our family members, it's crucial to remember that even when we fail, God's compassion is unfailing. And isn't it great that he is our portion for all of this grace?

Gasps

As with anything else in this life, when we make a decision to distance ourselves from our family members, we often have to contend with the opinions of others. As if we were not already subjected to the opinions of others enough, social media platforms came along and actually encouraged people to *publicly* share their like or dislike of the image of our lives, and to leave their comments behind when a simple emoji reaction is not enough. I don't know about you, but I am a millennial who joined Facebook in 2005, so I was never able to experience a period in my adult life where my peers did not feel entitled to offer their reactions to what was going on in my world. Today, it is not just your peers who feel compelled to offer their commentary, but people who you don't even know are not afraid to chime in as well.

If you are by chance thinking that I could simply choose not to actively participate in social media and share my life online . . . well, you would be absolutely correct. But what fun would that be? Besides, I am grateful for the life that I live, and I want to share my lived experiences with others, just the same as anyone else. My life, with the blessings therein, is evidence of my testimony.

Yet challenges tend to arise when people begin to notice that your lived experiences do not mirror their own or fit into the mold that our culture creates for us—and for our families. This is when they invite themselves to share their unsolicited thoughts and prayers for what they deem to be out of order in your life. They want to know why you were not with the family at the beach house or why your romantic partner suddenly disappeared from your timeline. They slide into your DMs (direct messages), asking why they have not seen your siblings in your photos for a while or wondering whatever happened to so and so. Though mostly well-intentioned, the barrage of comments and questions can harken back to the emotional whiplash that you have worked so hard to recover from.

Even though social media takes a lot of criticism for fueling the intrusive behavior of others, the reality is that this sort of prying or curiosity occurs within our offline social networks as well. Some of my most cringeworthy interactions involve gawks and gasps from others while at work, at church, or within other social settings. To make matters worse, these face-to-face reactions rob us of the shield of reading comments from behind our screens. These are the ones that can shake you the most. One minute you are at a holiday party snacking on chips and dip, and then the next thing you know, someone is asking, "Why is it that you never visit home for the holidays?"

This is precisely why New Year's Eve is my favorite holiday. Not only is it a natural marker of new beginnings; it is also the ending of the highly performative holiday season, also known as the time of year that is dedicated to gathering with loved ones and revisiting family traditions. During this stretch of the year, those of us who maintain some sort of distance from our families need to be prepared to deal with the expected emotions of craving connectedness and belonging, while also bracing ourselves for dealing with the people in our lives who do not understand our desire to do things a little bit differently. However, before you decide to delete all your social accounts or hunker down throughout the holiday season just to avoid social interactions, let me present to you that when we receive gasps from others, we are in the perfect position to testify about the goodness of God.

When others make it clear that they view your decision to distance from family as a source of lack or an excuse to mope, you are gifted with a chance to set the record straight. Your story is not about what you have lost but about the hope you have gained. These interactions provide the perfect opportunity to share about the healthy pain-preventing tactics that you have adopted and the peace that you enjoy because of them. Chances are, peace alone will sound appealing enough to nip any criticism and questioning in the bud.

And who better than you to be a beacon of light when others expect you to be burdened by grief? After learning how to cope with emotional whiplash and enduring family backlash, you are the perfect person to talk someone's ear off with your praises. As with David's song of thanksgiving after the Lord delivered him from a time of trouble, our interactions with others offer us the chance to share our testimony with everyone we know.

> I proclaim righteousness in the great assembly;
> see, I do not keep my mouth closed—
> as you know, LORD.
> I did not hide your righteousness in my heart;
> I spoke about your faithfulness and salvation;
> I did not conceal your constant love and truth
> from the great assembly. (Ps. 40:9–10)

Now, I won't lie to you—in the beginning, this may definitely be easier said than done. But as you continue to grow in the fullness and confidence of God, responding to the gawks and gasps of others will become much easier with time. If you need some ideas to get you started, here are some of my favorite ways to respond to comments and reactions from others that used to provoke feelings of guilt, shame, or regret about my familial circumstances:

- "I am so grateful for my cherished group of friends, who give me more love and support than I could ever ask for."
- "I actually find it pretty fun and exciting to create family traditions of my own."
- "I am overall more healthy, happy, and hopeful when I have distance from my family."
- "If even Jesus couldn't stay among his relatives for long, I know I'm in great company!"
- "Let he who is without family drama cast the first stone!"

The last two responses are for when you come across extra-judgey, churchy people who try to preach at you about the error of your ways. You know the ones.

Even though I am halfway joking about family-drama-free people casting the first stone, chances are that the ones who exhibit the most curiosity or noticeable reactions to your distance from family are likely to be the ones fighting their own battles behind the scenes. I cannot tell you how many times I have shared my newly established traditions or witty responses throughout the years, only to be contacted later by a friend who was inspired to create a boundary or distance of their own—and by doing so gained clarity and peace. And what joy those conversations bring.

A few years ago, I was sitting in an academic meeting with one of my former mentors, who said something so profound that it still sticks with me to this day. She said that often-times when people say they are inspired by something, what they really mean is that something they observed gave them permission to pursue the hidden desires in their heart that they were previously on the fence about.

To me, this is the embodiment of what it means to be salt and light. So many people are facing the same difficult dilemmas that you and I have faced, but they have buried their questions and concerns beneath a façade that feeds into cultural pressures and norms about family. When we turn our awkward interactions with others into opportunities to share our good news, we give them permission to pursue the hope we profess. We give them permission to take a step back from the needless suffering they may be experiencing in their own lives, allowing God to step in.

Grace

One of my favorite gospel hymns, written by Franklin Williams and sung by the Mississippi Mass Choir, is called "Your Grace and Mercy." It is one of those old-school songs that keeps the same beat as the lyrics run their course, allowing the choir to rock back and forth in a way that lulls you into a similar sway in your seat. The song is in that category of classic gospel music that instantly comforts your soul when you hear it. Songs in which the lyrics, melody, and beat are all designed to conjure up the emotions of overwhelming gratitude that leave you speechless and teary eyed. The refrain, which makes up the majority of the song's five minutes, goes like this:

> Your grace and mercy brought me through
> I'm living this moment because of you
> I want to thank you and praise you too
> Your grace and mercy brought me through

Although it is impossible to predict the extent to which you will experience emotional whiplash, family backlash, or gasps from outsiders in the aftermath of a family fallout, I cannot think of a better way to illustrate the response that you can expect from God. It does not matter if you were right or wrong, whether you feel forgiven or forgotten in your circumstances, or if people understand or support your decisions. You serve a God whose grace is sufficient. And just like the slow and steady beat of a classic gospel tune, God's grace is unwavering.

In Scripture, the apostle Paul boasts about God's grace in the same passage that he describes an ongoing battle with some sort of affliction (2 Cor. 12:6–9). Although it is never revealed what this affliction is, Paul refers to it as a "thorn in his flesh" given to torment him and prevent him from becoming too proud. He also reveals that though he prayed to the Lord three times for the affliction to be taken away, God's response to him was, "My grace is sufficient for you, for my power is perfected in weakness" (2 Cor. 12:9).

If you have experienced or are currently in the midst of a fallout with your family, you know what it's like to have a thorn in your flesh. And you know what it's like to pray repeatedly, asking for that affliction to be taken away. Even when you have made peace with your family's circumstances, and even when you have found hope by creating some distance or enforcing a boundary, the history of hardships and the wounds from the things we never saw coming will still remain. But those things are just one part of your story. And those parts can be used by God for good (Rom. 8:28). That's what happens when God's power is perfected in our weakness.

In fact, those parts of your story are being used right now. They have brought us here. We are living in this moment, meeting in these pages, and sharing in the hope we have in Christ simply because of God's grace. I don't know about you, but if my family had looked anything like the model family I used to cling to in my imagination, then I might never have been persuaded to dig into the depth of who God is or accept his invitation to live an abundant life. So I will gladly take this thorn—because without it, I may have never known God's grace.

BEAUTIFUL FUTURES

> LORD, you are my portion
> and my cup of blessing;
> you hold my future.
> The boundary lines have fallen for me
> in pleasant places;
> indeed, I have a beautiful inheritance.
>
> **Psalm 16:5–6**

Although it almost pains me to admit it, for the past few years I have been following a variety of interior design influencers on Instagram. In case you are wondering, yes, I have been influenced. I started off with simple motives when I bought my first home—I just needed to know how to style a semi-open floor plan. But over time, I went from being reluctantly influenced to becoming sincerely invested. The way bloggers are able to craft a story to pull you in and make a purchase is one of the most compelling types of marketing I have ever seen, and I teach courses in advertising for a living. So, anyway, I am officially invested in the lives of a few interior designers who post on Instagram.

Recently, one of my absolute favorite influencers shared that her mother had suddenly passed away. I was heartbroken for her. Prior to her passing, her mom would make appearances on her Instagram stories and posts, sharing hilariously corny mom jokes and doing adorable mom things, like feeding the dog the wrong type of food or sending one-line emails instead of texts. It was obvious that the bond between the two of them was incredibly strong. And I enjoyed being a witness to their healthy and loving mother-daughter dynamic.

So it made sense when my favorite influencer went missing from my timeline for a couple of weeks. In fact, I wondered if she would ever return to sharing videos of her shopping haul from HomeGoods or fun and quirky playdates with her pup after suffering such a devastating loss. Then one day she reappeared in better spirits and with a renewed sense of purpose. Turns out, the unexpected passing of her mother had resulted in her receiving a sizeable inheritance. With what she gained because of her loss, she was going to be able to take a year to travel the world—and she was going to bring us along on her account.

Thankfully, she is not one of those influencer types who paint a false picture of perfection in the face of loss; she's brutally honest about how much she is hurting. Her transparency is one of the reasons I am hooked on her account. Not only is she willing to be brutally honest about her hard-fought lessons on electrical wires and bathroom tiles; she's also honest and open about the hard-fought lessons of life, including how important it is to choose to make the most of your inheritance. And the urgency with which we should pursue a beautiful future.

Although most of my social media musings may come across as trivial, my prayer is that the image of a woman who chooses to chase hope in spite of suffering a devastating loss will resonate with you. Recently, I read that experiencing family estrangement or divorce is like living with a form of death that never dies. For many of us, our troubles with our loved ones can haunt us in this way. Like an unexpected death in the family, the thing that we never saw coming happens and changes us forever. Yet, though none of us would have chosen for our family's circumstances to turn out the way that they have, we can still choose to take the vision of family that we are grieving and exchange it for the hope of our beautiful inheritance.

At face value, it can be difficult to consider looking forward to an inheritance as being beautiful, especially since in order to receive one, you typically have to suffer a loss. But as believers, our inheritance is not connected to death; it is the promise of eternal life. In Scripture, the word *inheritance* is used to describe not only the tangible gifts of possessions and property, but also the earthly and spiritual gifts that God grants to us because we are his children. These are gifts that God offers as a means of procuring our hope and future not just in this life but also in the next (Eph. 1:21). When the apostle Paul writes about this to the church at Ephesus, he hopes to increase the understanding of the gifts of our adoption by explaining exactly how rich of a blessing our redemption is. There is so much good news packed into this passage of Scripture:

> I pray that the eyes of your heart may be enlightened
> so that you may know what is the hope of his calling,
> what is the wealth of his glorious inheritance in the
> saints, and what is the immeasurable greatness of
> his power toward us who believe, according to the
> mighty working of his strength. (Eph. 1:18–19)

I think what strikes me the most here is that Paul wants the people of God to understand that the riches of our glorious inheritance begin now. Our inheritance is not restricted to heaven. Remember all that talk about what it means to be co-heirs with Christ? Our adoption story does not simply end with a new birth certificate and inclusion in a family of believers. As heirs, we are granted a new identity in Christ and we are granted the fullness of life with him—that means the fulfillment of God's purpose, presence, and power in our lives *today*. Simply put, we don't have to wait until this life is over to enjoy all that God has for us.

God's plan for us is to know and enjoy a life so full that it overflows and impacts others. I cannot imagine any other interpretation of an abundant life (John 10:10). When we gain freedom from the mental, emotional, and spiritual baggage of needless suffering; when we are free of the abuse; and when we give up the desire to be the hero in our own stories, we gain the chance to simply live a life worthy of our calling (Eph. 4:1). And we can enjoy this life with or without our family of origin.

I would hate for you to deny yourself of this, because this is the good part. Why else would we endure the risk of emotional whiplash, family backlash, and the gawks and gasps of others, if not to enjoy a beautiful future? What's the point of all this if we do not choose to follow up with an abundant life? This is precisely the point of being a cycle breaker: to have something different—something more beautiful—to look forward to than the cycles we have seen. We choose to do things differently in order to preserve our light, increase our faith, and restore our hope. And we need each of these things, because sometimes enjoying your inheritance is easier said than done.

How to Enjoy a Beautiful Future

One might be tempted to think that enjoying a full and beautiful life would be easy to do, but oftentimes that's just not the case. For many people, enjoying the beauty of life after experiencing the darkness of life is like trying to quiet your mind after a long and busy day at work. Although you dreamt of returning home to peace and quiet all throughout the day, once you plop down on your bed, you can't seem to get your mind to feel at ease. Where is your mind instead? Still replaying the troubles of the day. Does this sound familiar to you?

Not being able to wind down at the end of a hectic workday is a very simple illustration of what it can feel like when you try to create a new life after experiencing some sort of trauma. You want a beautiful life. You tell yourself that you deserve a beautiful life. But for some reason, you are still impacted by the troubles of the past. The painful truth is that some of the things that have happened to us are so disruptive that they completely transform who we are and how we show up in the world. Even long after we have healed, we are still marked by our scars.

I want to take a moment to recognize that the word *trauma* might sound a bit scarier than what it actually is—our response to deeply distressing events. It can also be confusing because *trauma* is used to describe the thing that happened to us and also the way our body responds. For clarity, here I want to distinguish between *traumatic events* and *trauma responses*. Trauma responses occur when, instead of "forgetting," our mind develops its own ways to cope with what happened, often with the intent of preventing deeply distressing events from occurring again. These responses can manifest as emotional, physical, or behavioral symptoms that impact our daily lives. Our responses to traumatic events can be barely noticeable, as with an adult who sleeps with a nightlight on or a person who flinches whenever they are touched.

These types of responses are actually quite common, so I want to encourage you not to be too hard on yourself if they sound familiar. There are a number of different ways that the mental and emotional remnants of our past troubles continue to show up in our lives. For instance, when I decided to be intentional about pursuing a long-term romantic relationship, I discovered that the trauma of what my father did was very much present in my approach to dating. For me, trauma showed up in how I chose to trust—or not trust—men, and the way that I guarded myself against emotional and sometimes physical vulnerability.

As a child, I had no control over much of what happened in my life. So as I got older, I naturally developed protective responses to keep myself from experiencing future trauma. One day, I found myself blurting out to my current therapist that I was really struggling with romantic courtship. Just when I was beginning to go down the rabbit hole of how my past was ruining my hopes and dreams for the future, she hit me with a kick to the gut, per usual.

"I think you should consider your trauma a good thing," she told me. "It means that you are wiser and your instincts are sharper. You are not as naïve as other women about the bad things that happen in the world, and you are equipped with the wits that you need in order to prevent them from happening to you. You will never be in that position again."

Or, at least, that's how I remember it.

I will never forget that conversation because that perspective shift changed everything for me. For so long, I had moped around feeling as if I had a scarlet "T" tacked to the story of my life. And while I was grateful to have established some distance from the brokenness of the past, I could not quite figure out what to make of my present and future. Instead of embracing the newness of my life, I was stuck in a self-pity party in the present and pointing the finger at my past for making it so difficult to move on. I had never stopped to consider that it was my troubles that had prepared me for a beautiful future and equipped me with the wisdom and instincts I would need to procure it. My life wasn't difficult; it was simply different from what I was expecting. And, well, wasn't that the point?

When I walked away from that session, I had a new appreciation for the advice offered by James in Scripture, who writes that we should count our trials and suffering as joy: "Consider it a great joy, my brothers and sisters, whenever you experience various trials, because you know that the testing of your faith produces endurance. And let endurance have its full effect, so that you may be mature and complete, lacking nothing" (James 1:2–4).

I also had a new appreciation for romantic courtship. In case you were wondering how I feel about the woes of dating in my thirties, just know that I count it all as joy. Every bad date or failed relationship—and there have been plenty to go around—leaves me more mature and better prepared for my future love story than I was before, as all the hard things that happened with my family and our past have prepared me for my present.

Now might be a good time to remind you that nothing—absolutely nothing—gets wasted by God. Everything is used for good. Even our trauma. Regardless of where you currently stand with your family of origin, you can count it all as joy that the trials in your story have molded you and provided you with wisdom and preparation for the unique and beautiful life God has planned for you. If you are struggling to see the newness in your life as beautiful, here are a couple of questions you might consider:

- Am I struggling because my life is difficult or because it is different?
- In what ways is my life different because of my troubles?
- In what areas am I smarter, wiser, or more prepared for the future because of my unique story?
- How can my story be used for good?
- How can my story be used for the glory of God?

With the answers to these questions, you have the start of a blueprint that you can use to create something new and embrace a new way of showing up in the world. If you allow the trauma of the past to prevent you from moving forward with confident expectation, you run the risk of missing out on the fullness of life. Whatever happened to you—the awful things you witnessed, the hurt you felt, and the losses you have suffered—is not all there is. You have broken the cycle and things are different now.

You are different now.

You want a beautiful life.

You deserve a beautiful life.

And God's desire is for you to live one.

Take it from me, once you shift your perspective, the beauty of your life will slowly begin to come into focus. I cannot tell you how many times I have looked around and found myself overcome by tears of gratitude for the life that I am able to enjoy. I mean, honestly, sometimes when my son and I are just doing simple things around the house, like baking banana bread or sitting on opposite ends of the sofa watching our favorite TV shows, I want to pinch myself to be sure that I am not living in a dream. When I became a mother at nineteen years old, and a single mom the very next year, I was so fearful about what the future would look like for my family. At the time, I did not realize that my fear was grounded in a fairy-tale version of family that is impossible to obtain.

If you would have told a younger version of myself that one day I would have a house in the suburbs with rosebushes out front, a home office, and plenty of space for my son and our dog, Ray Charlie, to run around in the backyard, I probably would have looked at you as if you were speaking in a foreign language. And it's not that I am enamored by these material things; I am consistently taken aback by how incredibly content and fulfilled I am. And then it dawns on me that this is why I count it all as joy.

Can you believe that in the past I questioned if this type of life was even possible? And by "this type of life," I mean one in which I enjoy the stability and security of being healthy, happy, and whole. When you have endured hardships such as relational dysfunction, needless suffering, or living with the constant dread of everything falling apart, a life of safety and contentment starts to look a little too much like a Cinderella story.

At the risk of making my life sound about as perfect as the homes posted by interior design influencers online, I want to be clear that it is not. I don't share the details of my story to make it seem as though my life or family no longer has troubles. Just like bad dates, there are plenty of troubles to go around. But the difference is that now, my surrender is steadfast. I no longer try to force my family or myself to fit into an image fueled by a cultural obsession with perfection. I am no longer bound by the lies of family ties. Instead, I have chosen to create a different story of family—one that honors and glorifies God.

Freedom of Choice

I would like to officially go on the record debunking the myth that you can't choose your family. Not only is it untrue, but also the phrase just puts out really bad vibes. I don't think I've ever heard anyone say, "You can't choose your family," while making an encouraging point. The entire premise of the idea is that you are stuck in circumstances beyond your control that you must endure forever, and there is very little optimism to be found in that.

While we are on the topic, I also want to send a sneer toward the phrase "family ties." I mean, seriously, "ties"?! It wreaks of bondage. And with commonly used words and phrases like these, it is no wonder why so many of us spend years believing that we have to remain tethered to relationships or loved ones that harm us. To borrow a phrase from a Baptist pastor, I don't know about you, but my Bible says that Christ set us free so that we can *enjoy* our freedom (Gal. 5:1). So can we agree to do away with all that bondage talk already? Because if there's one thing I love about life, it is our free will.

We maintain the right to choose what we want in—or out—of our lives. This includes our families. Case in point: God chose me and you. And when we accept the call to salvation, we choose God. And if that's not enough evidence, we could simply revisit the ins and outs of the adoption process, which affords tens of thousands of families the option of choice each year. The point that I am trying to drive home to you right now is that you can absolutely, unequivocally choose people to join you in your efforts to create a new family story. And you should.

God made it very clear from the beginning that it is not good for us to live solitary lives (Gen. 2:18). We are designed to enjoy the benefits of community. Although it would be lovely if our families of origin were able to fulfill that need, strong relationships with loving friends and other believers are more than capable of standing in the gap in the event that our family ties become untethered—see what I did there? I often find myself deeply inspired by the many accounts of powerful friendships turned family in the lives of some of our favorite Bible characters.

Naomi anticipates living a life as a bitter widow after the death of her husband and sons, but her daughter-in-law Ruth offers a compelling account of devotion and declares that she will stick with Naomi until the day she dies (Ruth 1:16–17).

King David and Jonathan formed an instant bond upon meeting and made their friendship a covenant to the Lord (1 Sam. 20:41–42). Throughout his life, Jonathan prevents his own father, King Saul, from being successful in his attempts to kill David. After Jonathan dies, David takes in his son and raises him as his own.

The apostle Paul meets Timothy while on a missionary journey and gracefully steps into the role of his spiritual father and mentor. Over time, their bond grows, and they enjoy each other's companionship as they travel far and wide spreading the gospel, enduring hardship, being imprisoned, and more.

And perhaps my favorite story of all is the one about the crew of men who carried their disabled friend on a bed to be healed by Jesus (Luke 5:18–20). These friends are the embodiment of what I think of when I hear the phrase "ride-or-die." So much so that when they could not get to Jesus through the front door because of the crowd, they climbed on top of the house and lowered their friend down through the roof. These friends stepped in and did what their friend was unable to do for himself. Because of his friends, the man was placed in a position to receive a miracle.

The thought of a group of guys carrying a friend who could not carry himself probably sticks with me the most because it reminds me of my own amazing group of friends. I mean, seriously, I often feel like I have a sitcom-worthy group of friends, as unrealistic as that used to seem. Between my friends from graduate school, my book club, my small group, and my dedicated prayer partners, I have about a dozen or so women who support me through endless group chats and girls' nights. But they also support me through the hard stuff, too—the stuff that used to ding me with feelings of guilt, shame, or defeat if I did not have a family member around who could help me out, and when I could not help myself. Things like moving out of state with a kid in elementary school, buying my first home as a single woman, arguing with the car repair guy, dating in my thirties, or navigating the never-ending politics of being a Black woman in the academy.

These may sound like minor achievements to you, but they are major victories to me. In the past, facing any one of these hard things on my own would easily send me back to the "Why me?" and "I wish this had never happened" state of emotional whiplash. Navigating adulthood without the readily available support system of a tight-knit or expansive family structure can leave you feeling socially handicapped. But now, I barely even bat an eye before reaching out to a friend, knowing that they will have my back. If you can't tell, my friendships are a critical component of the pain-prevention strategy that minimizes the fallout of not enjoying the type of familial relationships that I often see in the lives of others. They are also an undeniable source of beauty in my life.

Cultivating a community of trustworthy friends and mentors is one of the most important things we can do as believers, especially for those of us with a complicated family story. Through our friendships, we enjoy companionship, protection, mentorship, advocacy, and spiritual guidance. But, above all, we experience the fullness of God's grace and mercy in how others care for us and seamlessly complement our strengths, weaknesses, and areas of need. This is the beauty of healthy relationships.

But there's just one catch. Unlike our families of origin, we are not granted the gift of beautiful friendships simply by being born. We have to work at them. As the Proverb says, in order to make friends, you have to first be friendly (Prov. 18:24). And that can be the hard part. (At least for me it was.) I certainly hope I did not lead you to think that I magically appeared in adulthood with sitcom-worthy friendships. Nope, I absolutely did not.

As it happens, one of the side effects of hiding your trauma from the world is that you often end up hiding yourself. I spent so much time building border walls around myself, so that people could not catch a glimpse into my world, that I managed to avoid spending almost any time learning about other people. As a result, the bulk of the insight that I had on how to be in relationship with other people was based on my experiences with my family members. And with such a limited sample size, it was not out of the ordinary for me to jump to the wrong conclusions about people based on even the slightest resemblance to someone who had hurt me in the past.

Those pesky trauma responses are not a respecter of persons. Whenever they see a red flag, they jump into action— that is, unless you intentionally set out to conquer them. This means getting rid of the scarlet "T" on your life and doing the challenging work of becoming friendly. After all, when you finally get the chance to meet the people who will eventually become a part of your chosen family, don't you want them to choose you too? If you desire to create a new family story, there are a few tactics I recommend you embrace.

Be Honest about What You Need

The first thing I had to do in order to pursue meaningful relationships was to admit that I needed other people. This tends to be a bit challenging because admitting that you are in need of someone or something can hit you right at the heart of your pride or point to a source of your deepest pain. So many of us who have endured family trauma or separation have had to develop maladaptive coping mechanisms that make it seem as though we have superpowers. We pride ourselves on being able to handle just about anything that comes our way without the help of anyone. By doing so, we just so happen to disregard the fact that maybe we would accept the help if we actually knew where to find it. I hate to break it to you, but this is often a trauma response developed after being let down by people you used to trust.

In my own life, I realized pretty quickly that I needed a community of support and wise counsel. In the aftermath of my mother moving out during the first year of my doctoral program, I faced a number of significant life events. I had to make important decisions, such as where I should live at the beginning of my career and how to approach shared custody with my son's father. These are big questions for anyone to face, and attempting to address them while relationships with my family members were on the mend was not easy to do.

In lieu of trying to figure everything out on my own—okay, let's be honest: I tried but failed miserably—I had to admit that I needed a crew to do life with. And so I went and found them. Taking a cue from one of my favorite movies, *Coming to America*, I started by going to church. (I have already shared just how life-changing joining my first small group was, and I have made being a member of some type of small group a continued priority; in addition, I try to serve on at least one ministry team and attend church socials or service events.) At that uncertain and transitional time in my life, I also made a point to connect with other people who were at similar points in their lives or shared similar experiences and interests. Enter my book club, professional organizations, alumni association, and the mom squad that camps around outside of school during pickup time.

In the beginning, this was a lot. Social anxiety can be a natural trauma response for people who have been subjected to emotional abuse, such as harsh criticism or ridicule. I always felt anxious about getting to know new people, because I worried how they would respond once they knew more of my story. I wish I would not have wasted so much time entertaining that fear, because the reality is that the super-ugly parts of my story rarely even rise to the surface now that I have peace. And whenever they do, I am reminded that I have curated an amazing group of people in my life who don't judge me, many of whom have stories with super-ugly parts as well—we all do.

Although my friends are amazing indeed, I have learned that there are some questions and predicaments that require the wisdom of an elder. After all, Scripture tells us that understanding comes with the length of our days (Job 12:12). You might be surprised to learn that I approached this need head on by simply asking elders if they could meet this need in my life. Of course, just like one might approach professional mentorship, I reached out to people in my life with whom I already had rapport. I have leaned on the parents of my friends, mothers in the church, and former college professors during moments when I felt like I needed parenting or a wise perspective. Rarely have I encountered reluctance while imparting their gracious words of wisdom.

Ultimately, once I was able to identify the areas in my life where I felt there was a need, it became increasingly easier for me to be intentional about curating my friendships and relationships around those needs. Once you take a moment to seek God and reflect on your own life, you may find that you have areas of need that you previously overlooked, such as clear communication, personal space, affection, emotional support, and so on. And this insight will allow you to make smarter choices about the family you are creating for yourself.

Unfortunately, since our unmet needs tend to shine a light on the troubles or trauma we have faced, we run the slight risk of experiencing some emotional whiplash. For example, reaching out to an elder for motherly advice can often surface some of my insecurities regarding my relationship with my mother. Whenever this happens, take heart in knowing that when you are intentional about recognizing your own needs, the devil has a much harder time taunting you with lies about what you lack. Besides, we have it written in Scripture that when we seek God first, all the things we need will be provided for us (Matt. 6:33). But first, we have to be honest enough to bring our needs to him.

Have Realistic Expectations for Other People

I am one of those people who have the annoying tendency to use expressions that repeat an idea in order to state the same idea plainly. I know you know what I am talking about— phrases like "It is what it is," or "Winners are going to win," or "Haters are going to hate!" While these sayings may sound simple-minded and redundant, I firmly believe in their profound ability to convey a state of acceptance. Some things just are the way they are. And you should know that here I am resisting the urge to justify our need for realistic expectations of other people with the simple phrase "People are going to people." But I know that sometimes having realistic expectations for people is hard to do, especially when you have been let down by people in the past.

This was perhaps one of the most challenging tactics for me to embrace while trying to build healthy, long-lasting relationships. In fact, you have probably gathered by now that for years I had a people problem. Oddly enough, I did not realize this until I started my career. In the office, I would find myself becoming easily frustrated with certain personality types or behaviors. Up until that point, I had never pictured myself as someone who had such a short fuse, but then again, being a career student meant that I had never had to work with so many people up until that point. And since we moved away from my mom's family when I was so young, I also missed out on the natural socialization that occurs when you get to hang out with uncles, aunties, and cousins on a regular basis.

Of course, at this point I had convinced myself that I actually enjoyed a life of relational minimalism. It never dawned on me that people were just being themselves; I thought everyone was making it a point to get on my nerves. I know that sounds awful. After a while, it felt awful too, which is how "dealing with people" became another topic of conversation with my new therapist at the time. This therapist, who I found after moving to Houston, was almost the complete opposite of my therapist from graduate school—she is a no-nonsense Black woman in her sixties who doesn't mind telling it to me straight. As soon as I shared my family history, she began nodding her head. "I see," she said. "You don't know what it is like to be around ordinary people."

Turns out, making a judgment call on people who have been in your life for a month or two, based on your experiences with the few people who have been in your life for its entirety, is simply unfair. Now, to be clear, there are some harmful behaviors and personality types that stick out to me from a mile away. I consider my discernment of those to be a part of my smarter and sharper instincts gifted by my trauma. But discernment is completely different from judging someone because they wear the same style of clothing as your parent or quote the same novel as your know-it-all sibling. Ordinary people need grace. And you need time to get a sense of who they are, beyond the preconceived notions that you are carrying from your past.

When you have been hurt, rejected, or abused by someone whom you cared for deeply, it is easy to find yourself wincing at even the slightest hint that someone new might hurt you in the same way. And it's easy to want to make people prove that they are 100-percent safe before you allow them into your life. Because of the fast-paced and judgmental culture we live in, we jump at the chance to quickly classify people in simple binaries like good or bad, sinner or saint, healthy or toxic. But these are impossible classifications when, in general, every person is made up of a bit of all the above.

Which brings me back to my original point: people are going to people. And there is very little we can do about this, besides learning how to live with them. People will hurt you and disappoint you, and they will mess up, but making a few mistakes is not the same as subjecting you to the abuse or harm that you may have experienced in the past. I can't stress how important it is to remember that. Because when your trauma response tells you to run at the slightest sign of danger, you are going to have to learn how to stick around and see if it is a false alarm.

And while you wait, pray for patience, wisdom, discernment, and a good judge of character. That is the only way we can hope to get reasonably good people to stick around. Only Christ can meet our standard of perfection, but you need people if you desire to create a new family story.

It is what it is.

Be Willing to Adopt New Behaviors

Be honest: how many times have you used the phrase "New Year! New Me!" only to make it to February and realize that the new you looks, sounds, and acts a lot like the *old* you? Don't worry, we have all been there. And what we realize every February is that in order to truly become a new you, you actually have to adopt new behaviors. It is easy to find yourself craving the comfort of familiarity, even when what is familiar is unhealthy. The same goes for creating new family stories or new family cycles. We have to resist the temptation to revert back to our old selves.

I will try to make this brief because you have probably heard this sermon preached before. The people of Israel are practically the poster children of declaring they wanted something new, only to change their mind when they had to adopt new behaviors, like living off a new type of food called manna (Num. 11). Doing new things was so hard that in their complaining they admitted they would have rather gone back to being slaves. Although their complaints might seem difficult to imagine now, their resistance to change is likely relatable.

Charting new territory might stretch you to the point of discomfort, but after a while, you will start to enjoy the benefits of your newfound mobility. This is the mindset I have embraced while raising my son. In the beginning, I struggled with finding my way, especially in light of all of the advice I received from grandparents and older siblings. But in the end, I knew I wanted to create a life for my son that I never had, so I had to do things that my parents and their parents had never done before.

I can admit now that my "new-age parenting tips" probably felt just as odd as they looked to everybody else when I was trying them out. When I was in graduate school, I made it a point to bring my son with me everywhere I went. I also read books to him around the clock—even some of my textbooks. I make it a point to tell him "I love you" literally every time he leaves the house. During his elementary school years, I made it a point to walk him in on every first day of school and introduce myself to his teachers. I ask him about his day every single time he comes home from school. I don't allow him to play with toy guns of any sort. I let him sleep in the bed with me periodically up until he got too big, at almost ten years old. (That was controversial!) And perhaps the newest new thing of them all is that I allow my son to talk to me as if he were "grown." Or at least that's what the old folks say. I simply call this having a conversation.

Thankfully, we have just entered his teenage years, and I am now reaping the benefits of all the new parenting behaviors I adopted throughout the years. I can tell you that without a doubt, I know I don't have to worry about my son experiencing most of the troubles or insecurities that I did as a child. And the ones he does run into are simply those that go along with being a kid. The point is, if you want to experience a family story unlike the one you have known, you have to do things differently than the way you have always done them.

Obviously, this doesn't apply to just parenting. I have had to adopt new behaviors in my finances, in my friendships, in my walk with Christ, and in many other areas of my life. In order to do this, I've had to do my research. I learn from observing others. I routinely pick up new books. I pose questions to mentors, experts, or people who I see embodying some of the qualities or experiences I desire. And I pray for the humility of a lifelong learner so that, like the apostle Paul, I will never arrive at the place where I believe I have figured it all out (Phil. 3:12–14). And though the learning curve might often throw me for a loop, I can tell you one thing: when I say, "New Year! New Me!," you better believe that I mean it.

All Things New

Before we all go riding off into the sunset, daydreaming about ways to create our new families and futures, I want to add one more thing. In all of your efforts to create a beautiful future, it is so important to remain hopeful about what God can do with your past. I would be remiss to explore all the new things that God can do in your life without mentioning how important it is to leave room for him to do something new in your family of origin as well.

As long as you are still breathing, you can be assured that your story is not finished, and the same goes for your loved ones. God is big enough and wide enough and deep enough to heal, restore, and sustain our broken or tainted relationships. Depending on your circumstances, reconciliation may be possible. And more so, reestablishing closeness with an estranged family member can be beautiful.

In Scripture, we see this play out in the story of the twin brothers Esau and Jacob (Gen. 25–33). Jacob was born clinging to the heel of his brother and with the personality of a natural trickster. Later in life, Jacob schemed with his mother to steal his older brother's birthright, resulting in a cruel divide among the family. Esau was angry and planned to kill his brother, so their mother told Jacob to flee. As a result, the brothers were estranged for many years.

Yet, in the years that they were apart, God was able to do work in them both. Jacob had repeated encounters with God that changed his character from that of a trickster to one of a dedicated servant and leader. In fact, at one point on his journey, he wrestles with the angel of the Lord and is given a new name, Israel, meaning a man who wrestles with God. As Jacob continues to wrestle with God both literally and metaphorically, he also prays about the status of his relationship with his brother. Finally, Esau's heart softens, and he is able to forgive Jacob. When they reunite, Jacob says that seeing Esau is like seeing the face of God. Although their reconciliation does not lead to a lifelong adventure that movies are made of, the brothers do receive the praiseworthy gift of finally being at peace.

While not every family story will have a similar ending, this story of reconciliation certainly gives me hope. You might be Esau in your story, or you might be Jacob. On either side, there is a pathway to procuring a greater future. I love how Esau's journey demonstrates that maintaining a boundary or distance does not mean that you have to harbor unforgiveness. If you were wronged by a loved one, you might find that taking the space and spending some time apart does wonders for lessening the hurt you used to feel.

And if you were the relative who caused the divide, there's plenty to learn from Jacob's many confrontations with God. The work that God is doing in you may get messy and it may take time, but with prayer and faith, you will find that God will complete the work that he began in you (Phil. 1:6). And when he does, that is the perfect time to put away your guilt and shame and reach out to see if you can make amends.

Regardless of where you fall on the side of conflict in your family's story, if it is your heart's desire to pursue reconciliation, you can simply adopt the same mindset that you would for creating a new family in order to restore relationships with your family of origin. Be honest about what you need. Have realistic expectations for people. And be willing to adopt new behaviors. You may be encountering the same family you were born into, but every day presents new opportunities for God to transform and reinvigorate your lives and legacies anew.

OVERCOMERS

> They conquered him
> by the blood of the Lamb
> and by the word of their testimony;
> for they did not love their lives
> to the point of death.
>
> **Revelation 12:11**

I don't know about you, but in the Black families I know there is an unspoken rule that "what goes on in this house, stays in this house." Actually, it is not an unspoken rule at all—more like one that is reinforced so vehemently that after a while it no longer has to be said. As soon as you are old enough to repeat the colorful words and phrases of your parents' or older siblings' conversations on the playground, you are taught the family code of silence—and to fear the consequences of breaking it.

Granted, now that I am a Black mother raising a Black son, I get it. I understand how when Black people tell our truths, we run the risk of suffering even graver consequences in the outside world compared to others. I understand that we might hesitate to tell our truths because they may sound too similar to stereotypes used to justify generalized mistreatment. I understand that sometimes when we tell our truths, people may question our motives or call us liars. And I understand that sometimes when we grasp for the guts to tell our truths, our words fall on deaf ears and we wonder why we ever opened our mouths in the first place. But I never realized how much needless suffering this saying could cause until years into my adulthood.

Because I feared the consequences, I never told the truth about the circumstances surrounding my childhood or the various traumas my family had endured. And because of my silence, I had created a world in my head that was much darker and lonelier than it should have been. What happened in our house stayed in our house, and then it stayed in me long after I left our house. It then remained in me until it felt as if our secrets were pulling me apart at the seams. If you have ever kept a family secret, or simply refrained from sharing your truth, I am sure you know just how treacherous of an existence it is to suffer in this way.

Have you ever stopped to think about how odd it is that we are so afraid of sharing our stories that the simple act of telling the truth is often described as an act of bravery? Of course, here I mean *simple* in theory, not in practice. Because some truths are harder to tell than others. In practice, telling hard truths often gets conflated with weakness, or retaliation, or betrayal. Consequently, the very worst parts of our humanity are hidden in a shroud of secrecy and secured tightly by fear. And this is exactly what our enemy seeks.

Isolation

Skepticism

Comparison

Shame

Mistrust

These are the tools in his arsenal, and every moment we bury our truths behind well-crafted and well-intended lies of omission, we are falling prey to a plan designed to harm us and others. The strategy of this scheme, in particular, is to prevent us from sharing our stories because of what happens on the other side of our silence.

Nothing will change a person more than the moment when they hear someone else's story and their insides start to tremble. In that moment, something cracks, and hope intrudes into the space where the pit of fear typically resides. Hope that maybe they are not as alone as they thought or as out of their mind as they once feared. Hope that because someone else was bold enough to share their truth, there might be a precedent for their own truth to be accepted by others. Hope that suggests that maybe, just maybe, their life does not have to remain the way that it is. The plan of the enemy is to prevent people from having a moment when they can hear someone else's truth and ask, "You too?" Because that is the moment that changes everything. This is the power of our testimony.

Reasons to Testify

Oddly enough, at the same time we were being raised not to talk about what was happening behind closed doors, we were also forced to sit quietly through the hour-long part of church service that was dedicated to giving testimonies. If you were not raised Baptecostal like me (Baptist + Pentecostal), this part of the service was when people were invited to grab the microphone and share with the congregation what God had been up to in their lives. Every. Single. Week.

And, boy, did those praise reports roll in. Evictions overturned. New jobs. Miraculous healings. Marriages restored. You name it. Sometimes people would even testify about the tiniest wink they received from God during the week, like an answered prayer to let their full tank of gas last until the next payday or that they might be able to finally get a full night's rest. If you ask me, the reason why this part of the service lasted so long was because sharing good news tends to be infectious, especially when it gives people something to believe in. It was not uncommon for the testimony hour to turn into a full praise and worship break, followed by an inevitable invitation to Christ.

I use the word *inevitable* here because when we tell the truth, our stories point people to God. Whenever a testimony goes forth about how God made a way for the rent to be paid, someone who is facing eviction feels a stirring in their spirit. When someone rejoices that their child has returned home, a mother who has been staying up all night praying for their child swells with expectation. These nudges in the spirit plant seeds of hope and invite people to try Jesus. But we won't get the honor of sharing in the harvest if we never testify.

When we hold back the ugly parts or put forth a watered-down version of our story, we rob people of the opportunity to see what God has truly done in our lives. For every part of your story that you think is too grim to tell, there is someone out there in the midst of the very same thing you are surviving, or worse. This is why Scripture instructs us to put off falsehoods and tell each other the truth (Eph. 4:25). As the body of Christ, it is our truth-telling that allows us to enjoy unity through honest, loving relationships with one another. When we tell the truth, we triumph over the secrecy and fear that had us bound. And we invite others to do the same.

As believers, we dedicate a good bit of time to preaching about the power of what Jesus did on the cross, but not nearly enough on the power of sharing our stories. I need you to believe me when I say this: Your story is powerful. So powerful that it puts fear in the bones of our enemy. So powerful that it is listed alongside the blood of Jesus in a twofold tactic for defeating the devil (Rev. 12:11). And so powerful that it secures a twofold win: freedom for you and hope for others who hear what God has done in your life.

When we tell our stories, we block the enemy from being successful in one of his oldest schemes. You know, the one that bolsters itself on lack of knowledge and isolation in order to plant seeds of doubt and separation from God. This tactic works best when no one else is around to tell a different story, because then we are primed for manipulation. The enemy uses a blank slate to build a narrative wrought with lies, convincing you to question the character of God, or if he is even real. This is the same old scheme he used on Eve in the Garden of Eden and the one he tried to use on Jesus when he was alone in the desert.

The difference is that when Jesus was tempted in the desert, he used the written Word of God as his line of defense. For every lie the devil hurled at him, Jesus had a verse of Scripture to defend himself. He could not be persuaded by lies because he knew the true story of God. Though it would be nice if we were all able to defend ourselves against the devil's deceit as skillfully as Jesus, that is not the reality of our fallen world. Many people are introduced to God by stories first and then get to know him through Scripture. As the apostle Paul writes:

> How, then, can they call on him they have not believed in? And how can they believe without hearing about him? And how can they hear without a preacher? And how can they preach unless they are sent? As it is written: **How beautiful are the feet of those who bring good news.** (Rom. 10:14–15— emphasis in original)

When we tell our stories, we bring the good news to the lives of others. Consider how different my story would be if I had never heard the stories from that group of women in my first small group so long ago. When I heard women speaking openly about the brokenness they were experiencing in their marriages and families, it literally changed the course of my life. Before I walked into that room, I felt completely alone. Even now, it pains me to remember how I was craving true connection and chasing it in broken relationship after broken relationship. How I was using alcohol to create a version of myself that felt safe enough to share with the world. And how I had convinced myself that the life I wanted was not available for people like me.

In that room, I discovered that I was not the exception to the rule. Messy families and ugly truths are not rare deviations from the natural order of things; they *are* the norm. As awful as this all sounds, learning that I was not alone was the good news. If you recall, I was initially the person who unleashed gawks and gasps when these women started to share. But the women in that group were not downcast and defeated; they had stories of faith that I desperately needed to hear. They showed me that even when you are in the midst of turmoil that feels all bad, God is still good. In the end, it was their truths that gave me permission to cast off fear and shame and finally tell mine. And once I did, I knew I would never be the same.

That moment is one of my greatest memories of having a personal encounter with God. I had prayed so long for an end to the hopelessness I was feeling, and I received it in a community built on telling the truth. Whenever I find myself leaning into a cultural ideal of perfection—family, faith, or otherwise—I cling to the memory of those women and their stories, and the day I learned that what I thought I knew was not all there is. With Jesus, there is so much more.

The hope I found in that room is why I tell my testimony every chance I get. Because I know how high the stakes are. I know that there are people who are suffering in silence, battling loneliness, and waging what feels like a war for the future of their lives. And they need to know what grace looks like in action. They need to see boldness in exchange for brokenness and hope for all the ways that they are hurting. They need an encounter that points them toward God.

That is precisely what I set out to offer in these pages. I did not share the ugly parts about my father, my family, my childhood, and my trauma because I was running out of space in my journal. I did not tell my story because I was angry, or hurt, or seeking revenge. Nor did I tell my story here because I felt my therapist had heard it enough. I did it because I know—without a shadow of a doubt—that there is someone who will read these pages and feel the weight of hopelessness begin to melt away. I can feel it in my innermost being, and I have been praying for you. Because there is someone in your life who is waiting on you to share yours.

Believe me, I know the thought of it is scary. But I want to encourage you and tell you that there is freedom—so much freedom—on the other side of telling your truth. I graciously offer myself as a living testimony. I told you from the beginning that I was trembling, but I kept writing anyway. Then the God of all comfort came and comforted me. The beauty of it is that he did this so that I might be able to comfort you (2 Cor. 1:3–7). I don't know about you, but this is one cycle I have no desire to break—a cycle that comforts others when they need it the most. A cycle that starts with telling the truth.

Now, you don't have to go yelling your story from the rooftop. And I am not asking you to write a book, or start a blog, or become an Instagram influencer. (Although you certainly can do those things too—Lord knows the world needs it.) I simply pray that when the chance comes, you will remember my story and you will be brave.

ACKNOWLEDGMENTS

The Baptecostal girl in me can't start any testimony without first saying, "Giving honor to God, who is the head of my life," simply because I know that without God, the blessing that is my story and the ability to write it down on paper would not be possible. Thank you, God, for saving me. This book is the result of God showering me with love and grace in the form of relationships with family members, friends, mentors, and loved ones who were divinely appointed to walk alongside me in this life.

To my son, Omari, I cannot adequately express how having you join me in this world dramatically transformed my life, my purpose, and my heart. Every day, you create new meaning for what family is and what family can be, and you breathe new life into parts of me that were previously bruised. You have inspired me and cheered me on as I have gone first down so many beaten paths, eagerly clearing the way for you. I am forever grateful that God chose me to be your mom and that we get to do life together.

To my mother, Glenda, and my siblings, Alison, Arica, and Basil Jr., the imperfections of our story reveal the extent of God's grace and hand upon our lives. I'm constantly in awe of your collective and individual strength and resilience and know that everything I am is because I am Glenda's daughter and the youngest of her four children, with each of your shoulders to stand upon, and a generation of nieces and nephews to lead down new paths. Thank you for everything—especially you, Mama, who always told me that regardless of our circumstances, I could still do and be whatever I dreamed.

To my sitcom-worthy group of all-star friends and members of my chosen family, words could never express the depth of my gratitude. To Justin, Stephanie and Brandon, Phylicia, Loren, Marcie, Stacie, Cynthia, Tiffany, Nicole, Sherra, Anika, Annessa, Brittney, and the rest of my small group members past and present—thank you for your prayers, encouragement, Bible studies, reminders, group chats, pep talks, hugs, laughs, tears, and friendship. You all have expanded my view of family and love in boundless ways.

Thank you to my prayer warriors and mentors—Julie, Thalia, and Clarissa—for your spiritual covering and the ways that you have sown into my ministry and life, especially you, Clarissa, who financially contributed to my writing goals on a whim one morning because God told you to. I am so grateful for your "yes" and your heart to serve others.

I am also thankful for the impactful, life-changing work of mental health professionals and advocates, including my own longstanding therapist, Toni, and all the others who have helped me work through the conflicting thoughts and emotions that come along with being first. And for my church home, Hope City, for introducing me to the powerful *Freedom* curriculum and small group that brought further clarity to the power and purpose of my testimony.

Last, thank you to the team at Leafwood Publishers, led by Jason Fikes, who immediately expressed support for the idea behind this book and continually affirmed that I should be the person to write it. You all have helped me take this message from my heart to the page, and I am excited to see how lives will be changed because of your guidance and support, including my own.